DIGITAL SWORD

How To Study and Prepare a Sermon with Bible Software

DR. JOHN DAVID FALLAHEE

Copyright © 2025 by Dr. John David Fallahee

Book Cover by Kate Fallahee

All rights reserved. No part of this publication may be reproduced, distributed or transmitted in any form or by any means without prior written permission.

Printed in the United States of America

Published by Digital Sword • Green Bay, WI

www.DigitalSword.org

Subject Headings:
RELIGION / BIBLICAL STUDIES / EXEGESIS & HERMENEUTICS

Unless otherwise stated, Scripture is taken from the King James Version.

LearnLogos.com
2nd Edition
ISBN 978-1-7337265-4-2

Dedicated to my LearnLogos.com customers:

Your passion for knowing God, His Word,

and His Will inspires me every day

to love my Savior Jesus Christ more deeply,

to serve His Body, the Church more faithfully,

and to handle His Word more accurately!

Thank you for your support, prayers,

patience, and encouragement!

*"Successes, failures, tragedies, and triumphs of the past
are either idols of the present
or wisdom for the future."*

— Dr. John David Fallahee

TABLE OF CONTENTS

CHAPTERS

WHAT'S IN THE BOOK? vi

BEFORE YOU PREACH, WORSHIP! 1

FINDING THE TREASURE IN THE TEXT 57

REMOVING THE VEIL OF BABEL, PART 1 95

REMOVING THE VEIL OF BABEL, PART 2 121

HOP, SKIP, AND JUMP 147

OPENING UP THE TIME CAPSULE 167

SEEING THE FOREST AND THE TREES 187

DOUBLE TAKE 211

VIRTUAL REALITY: ILLUSTRATING IN MULTISENSORY MODE 233

LIVING PROOF: INCARNATING THE LIVING WORD 261

INGREDIENTS TO INGESTION: IS YOUR MESSAGE A MEAL, MORSEL, OR JUST EMPTY CALORIES? 287

TICKLING EARS TO TRAINING HEARTS: WHAT KIND OF MESSAGE ARE YOU COMMUNICATING? 337

A ROSE BY ANY OTHER NAME WOULD SMELL AS SWEET! 359

DROP ANCHOR! DEALING WITH DEEP AND DIFFICULT PASSAGES 377

GOING MOBILE 397

GOD, YOU, & AI: BIBLE STUDY & SERMON PREPARATION 409

ABOUT THE AUTHOR 427

INTRODUCTION
WHAT'S IN THE BOOK?

CONGRATULATIONS!

You are about to embark on a wonderful learning journey to know God and His Word. I'll keep this short so that you can get started immediately.

HOW THE BOOK IS ORGANIZED

Nearly every chapter has eight sections; they are as follows:

1. Purpose: What you will learn in the chapter.
2. Preparation: This introduces the chapter's key ideas.
3. Instruction: You will be provided with instructions on how to improve your Bible study and message preparation.
4. Application: We will walk you through two example passages (Psalm 103:1-5, Matthew 8:23-27).
5. Presentation: You will find a link to online video training to further your learning on how to study the Bible with your computer.
6. Summary: We'll review what you have learned,

including goals, strategies, tactics, pitfalls, and warnings.

7. Excel Still More: We will give you a series of questions for self-evaluation. It's like having a personal coach.

8. Recommended Books: We'll list critical resources to help expand your digital library.

HOW TO USE THIS BOOK

We recommend studying the two passages provided in the book. This approach is the easiest way to follow along and learn. Consider this as a hands-on course. We'll walk you through key concepts and help you apply them practically. Check out our supplemental videos to help you along the way at www.DigitalSword.org.

I pray that together, you will improve your study of the Bible and communication of the Scriptures to others. You will also grow in Christlikeness and closeness to our Savior and Heavenly Father, yielding to the Holy Spirit.

CHAPTER ONE

BEFORE YOU PREACH, WORSHIP!

"Saying, Father, if thou be willing, remove this cup from me: nevertheless not my will, but thine, be done."

— Jesus the Word of God, Luke 22:42

PURPOSE

Learn to integrate prayer into your Bible study and sermon preparation.

PREPARATION

It is a privilege to answer the call of God as His ambassador to proclaim His transforming Gospel for the forgiveness of sin. Consider those responsible for accurately handling His Scripture on behalf of His people "week-in" and "week-out," knowing as they teach and preach, they will incur a stricter judgment (James 3:1).

Currently, you may not be leading a congregation, a Sunday school class, or even a small Bible study; but that does not change the fact that it is crucial to handle God's Word with the utmost precision (2 Timothy 2:15). It is in this tension and hard work between discovering, knowing, and applying Scriptures that is the excellent adventure our Savior invites each of us! As you learn and obey, you will grow, and then you will be able to help others be fruitful in the Lord. As we present the glorious truths of God's Word to others in these moments, we find the reason, motivation, and desperate need for prayer.

You may be wondering how Bible software can help you pray. The answer is that it can't. No technology can receive prayer requests, intercede on behalf of you and others, compose spirit-filled prayers, pray without ceasing, and ensure that God honors such prayers. No computer program or artificial intelligence-based software should be a substitute for real people praying. Nothing can replace intimate and vital time alone with

God by a child of God.

Five Critical Prayers

Five critical prayers should precede and saturate your Bible study and sermon preparation. They are as follows:

1) Pray for Illumination

Call upon God to help you understand His word. Acknowledge your helplessness and dependence on Him for insight.

2) Permit the Biblical Text to Judge You

When you study the Bible, it is critical that you remain tenderhearted toward the Lord and His Word. If there is a sin to confess, do not delay your repentance. If thinking needs to change, renew your mind with the mind of Christ. Remember, you can only grow up to the point of your disobedience.

3) Plead God to Apply the Text Immediately to Your Life

Seek the Lord and ask Him to provide an opportunity to

apply Biblical truth to your life tangibly and practically. It usually comes as a test, so be on alert! It may also come through observation, meditation, or even reflection. Reviewing or memorizing the Scriptures daily can be helpful, being mindful of God's word for every situation.

4) Petition on Behalf of Your Audience

Intercessory prayer keeps us humble and aware of the needs of others around us. We become less self-centered. Since your message intends to edify others, you will need God's help directing your studies to ensure that what you teach and preach meets the hidden spiritual needs of those listening.

5) Pray that God is Glorified

1 Corinthians 10:31 reminds us that whether we eat, drink, or whatever we do, all is for the glory of God. Therefore, seek to exalt God through the whole process, from praying to proclaiming.

Additional Thoughts on Prayer

Praying through a Biblical passage to study and prepare a message differs from other types of praying. I'm sure you've encountered one or more acronyms listed below to structure and guide your prayers.

Table 1. Prayer Acronyms

ACTS	IOUS	PRAY	PRAISE	PUSH	ASK
Adoration	Incline	Praise	Praise	Pray	Ask
Confession	Open	Repent	Repentance	Until	Seek
Thanksgiving	Unite	Ask	Adoration	Something	Knock
Supplication	Satisfy	Yield	Intercession	Happens	
			Supplication		
			Eternal Results		

As helpful as these acronyms may be to guide you in praying, they cannot help you with the spiritual demands made on you as you work diligently to understand a Biblical passage to nourish your soul and those you teach and shepherd. So, before we jump into the Bible software, let's zero in on the foundation and answer the question, "How do I pray for studying, leading, teaching, and preaching the Word of God to myself and others?"

There is no shortage of helpful books on prayer, and at the end of this chapter, you will find a brief list of suggested books on prayer for your enrichment and growth. However, before you purchase or download another book or resource, let's look to our Savior, who modeled the praying life and taught us how to pray.

Below are seven essential principles for guiding and improving your prayer life so that you can grow in faithfulness to God, His Word, and His Will. These principles result from studying all the prayer passages of Jesus in the Gospels. Let us together concisely examine the prayer life of Jesus.

Seven Key Principles of Prayer

Principle #1 – Any Time is a Good Time to Pray

Jesus did not use formulas or repetitious prayers when praying. He prayed often and at various times, straightforwardly conversing with His Father.

A. Pray Often

The underlying Greek tenses of the verbs in these Biblical texts emphasize prayer was a customary and habitual practice of Jesus (Luke 5:16, Mark 1:35).

B. Pray at Different Times

Because Jesus prayed often, we find Him praying—before dawn, during daylight, after sunset, and sometimes all night. Regardless of the circumstances, Jesus always prayed in the Spirit, being alert with all perseverance and petition (Ephesians 6:18), (Mark 1:35, Matthew 14:23, Luke 6:12).

Principle #2 – Any Place is a Good Place to Pray

The second principle of prayer is that neither people nor

your location should interfere with prayer and worship. Throughout Jesus' ministry, He found a place to pray despite the constant demands of the people. On some occasions, this required Jesus to withdraw entirely from people. In other situations, He departed with several or more of His disciples. Other times, He remained with individuals and prayed in their presence. We also read that Jesus was alone, and although the Scriptures do not always mention Him praying, because of Jesus' pattern of prayer, we can deduce that He was praying in His solitude.

A. Find Solitude

There are several examples where Jesus withdrew to be alone and pray. For example, the temptation by the devil in the wilderness (Luke 4:1, Matthew 4:1, Mark 1:12). We can assume that Jesus prayed throughout this temptation, although the Scriptures do not explicitly mention prayer. A second example would be when Christ withdrew from Galilee after the news of John the

Baptist's murder (Matthew 14:1–14, Mark 6:14–52). Before His betrayal by Judas, Jesus withdrew to Mount Olivet, most likely to pray alone (Luke 21:34–38). Regardless of circumstances and what was yet to occur, Jesus prioritized being alone in prayer with God the Father.

B. Prayer with Friends

We see Jesus bringing along several companions for prayer. One example is at the Mount of Transfiguration mentioned in Luke 9:28–36. Another example would be the high priestly prayer of Jesus in the upper room in John 17:1-26. Once, Jesus rebuked His disciples for interfering with His desire to lay hands on the children for prayer blessings (Matthew 19:13-15).

C. Pray in Public Places

The Lord Jesus Christ would pray before a large crowd and publicly address God the Father. It was to demonstrate the unique relationship between Himself and God, His Father. For example, in Matthew 11:20-30, Jesus praises His Father in prayer before the multitudes for those who believed despite the unrepentant cities of Chorazin, Capernaum, and Bethsaida. In John 11:1–44, Jesus thanked God the Father with a public prayer before raising Lazarus from the dead.

Principle #3 – Pray for All Decisions and Events

Jesus validates the need to seek guidance in prayer in anticipation of upcoming decisions and events. Seeking God's wisdom (James 1:5-8) must never be neglected regardless of how big or small the decision or event.

A. Pray Before Significant Decisions

One of the more remarkable passages is Luke 6:12-16, in which Jesus prays through the decision to choose the twelve apostles. We can conclude that Jesus communed with the Father in a specific prayer about a single decision, even setting aside the priority of sleep.

B. Pray Before Significant Events

In one of the most revealing passages into the mind and heart of Christ regarding His death on the cross, we see three prayers by the Lord Jesus Christ at Gethsemane (Matthew 26:36-46, Mark 14:32–42, Luke 22:39–46). Here, we see Jesus withdrawing with several close disciples and then withdrawing from them to pray alone. We see how Jesus prayed concerning His death on the cross for our sins. In agony, Jesus prayed fervently. Jesus models for us how to pray in the most difficult of circumstances.

Principle #4 – Pray Throughout the Ministry

In the trench work of ministry, where people demand attention, you must not neglect prayer. One must discover the balance between prayer's primacy and the ministering to people. But only through prayer can that balance be found and maintained. Whether Jesus is being baptized, discussing the death of a loved one, or even being interrupted by inquiring individuals, He demonstrates the balance of ministering to others and praying. His ministry reveals a dependence on prayer.

A. Jesus Prays at the Beginning of Ministry

In Luke 3:21-22, we see Jesus praying, heaven opens, and the Holy Spirit descends upon Him in bodily form like a dove. Between the baptism of Jesus and the temptation in the wilderness by Satan, we see Jesus inaugurating His ministry with prayer.

B. Jesus Prays During Difficult Times

In John 11, we read about the death and resurrection of Lazarus. The words Jesus prayed for Lazarus to rise from the dead are not in the Scriptures. However, we read in John 11:41-42 that Jesus thanked God the Father in the crowd's presence for hearing His prayer before raising Lazarus. As the people were mourning Lazarus' death, Jesus was grieving, yet He prayed. Learn from Jesus. He was continually praying, no matter how busy or distressed.

C. Jesus Prays at Busy Times

The Passover before Jesus' crucifixion was fast approaching, and He was answering questions from the Greeks in John 12:20-50. As Jesus taught the people that He must die, He petitioned God the Father to glorify the Father's name. After His prayer, the voice of God His Father speaks forth from heaven for all to hear (John 12:28). It is important to note that although Jesus is busy ministering to the people and Jesus Himself is grieving, Jesus prays not for Himself but for the glory of God.

Principle #5 - Prayer is the Concluding Activity

At the close of ministering to others, you must pray. One must reflect on the blessings, successes, and failures and then come to God the Father humbly with adoration, confession, and thanksgiving. Do not be tempted to neglect prayer.

A. Jesus Prayed After Feeding the 5000

It is humbling to note that even after a significant event

or miracle, Jesus allocates time to pray. In this incident, He sent the disciples away in a boat so that He could go to the mountain to pray (Matthew 14:23, Mark 6:46, John 6:15). Although exhausted from ministering to others, Jesus always found the strength to pray when the activities were over.

B. Jesus Prayed After the 70 Returned

In Luke 10:21-22, the seventy disciples Jesus sent out earlier (Luke 10:1) return rejoicing. Christ expresses divine joy in a public prayer of praise to God the Father. Christ manifests to us the priority of prayer and worship after ministering to others.

Principle #6 – Pray for Your Enemies

The Lord Jesus Christ portrays the principle of prayer in suffering and persecution like no other individual in the Bible or all of history. We see that under the severest of trials, prayer permeates His substitutional, sacrificial suffering for sin at the height of His persecution and pain on the cross. On the cross, the

Scriptures reveal seven sayings of Jesus, of which three are specific prayers.

A. Commencement of the Crucifixion

Jesus utters the following words, recorded in Luke 23:34, as the first saying on the cross, "Father, forgive them, for they do not know what they are doing." This intercessory prayer to God the Father was on behalf of His tormentors. Jesus' perfect example, despite intense pain, shows us how to pray at the inauguration of our trials. Jesus Christ, despite the injurious nature of the cross, looks past His immediate and painful circumstances and commits to prayer for the needs of His ignorant enemies.

B. Continuance of the Crucifixion

The fourth saying of Jesus on the cross is in Matthew 27:46, "Eli, Eli, lama sabachthani?" that is, "My God, My God, why have You forsaken Me?" This prayer, in the form of a question, looks back to Psalm 22. This solemn prayer reveals Jesus' anguish at being separated from God the Father for the first and only time in eternity, because of His sin-bearing (Isaiah 52:14-53:12). The fact that Jesus is praying while suffering for sins He did not commit should compel us to pray during intense moments of persecution and unjust suffering.

C. Conclusion of the Crucifixion

In Luke 23:46, we read, "Father, into your hands, I commit my spirit." The seventh and final saying of Jesus looks back to Psalm 31:5, consummating with prayer the completion of His cross-work to atone for sin. This prayer is a reminder that when the end is near, pray!

Principle #7 – Pray for One Another

Jesus models the principle of intercessory prayer. Although most of Jesus's intercessory prayers are not in the Bible, the Scriptures reveal that Jesus regularly interceded for people.

A. Prayer for Peter

In Luke 22:32, we discover Satan had requested to sift Peter like wheat. However, we read that Jesus had prayed for Peter earlier. Although we do not know when He prayed, it reveals that Jesus never lost sight of others and their needs amid the demands and pressures of life and ministry.

B. Priestly Prayer

In John 17:1-26, which takes place in the upper room before Jesus' betrayal, we have the most extended prayer of Jesus in the New Testament. The Lord Jesus is with the apostles. Jesus had washed their feet (John 13:1-20), the Passover meal had concluded, the Lord's Supper was instituted (Matthew 26:26-29), Judas had left to betray Jesus (John 13:21-30), and right before they sang a hymn and departed, Jesus took time to pray. Not only did Jesus pray for the soul-saving work He was to carry out on the cross, but He also prayed for the disciples and us, future believers. These petitions were not about wealth, prestige, or worldly influence. Jesus interceded on behalf of the disciples and future believers to God the Father for all of us to be kept from evil and the evil one. He prayed for us to be holy in a sinful world. He sought in prayer for us to be eligible for service and to be delivered safely to their heavenly home.

What can we conclude?
Life has its ebbs and flows, but prayerful communion with God the Father must be a constant for every born-again believer. To prioritize prayer in a busy schedule, one must pray before, during, and after all activities. It should not matter if you are in a season of peace, prosperity, painful trials, or even persecution. Never cease praying and petitioning on behalf of others.

Jesus exemplified this pattern throughout His ministry, whether alone, before few, or before many. Even though we have a few examples of the words Jesus prayed, His prayer life reveals that prayer was His priority. His example is sufficient to compel us to examine the priority of prayer in our lives. Let us not forget that Christ was sinless; He had a perfect relationship with the Father, yet He made prayer a priority. May you and I bow the knee before God our Maker and do the same.

Prayer Beyond the Life of Jesus

When you explore the topic of prayer in the Bible beyond Jesus's prayer life and examine all prayers from Genesis to Revelation, a fascinating pattern emerges. All genuine, God-honoring prayer reflects God's glory. The acronym REFLECT reveals this pattern. Each step in the tables below explains the acronym in more detail. When we pray, we need to R.E.F.L.E.C.T. the glory of God in prayer.

With these prayer principles, we can enrich our prayer time and rightly guide our prayers to ensure that we will never grow cold or indifferent to our Lord, His Word, or His will. If you wish to learn more about this method, please see my published book on prayer, REFLECT the Glory of God in Prayer, at Amazon or visit my website: LearnLogos.com/reflect. Here is a summary of these praying principles organized into seven steps.

Table 2. REFLECT Method of Prayer - Step 1

REMEMBER THE GLORIES OF GOD (STEP 1)
Moses: Desire to see the glory of God (Exodus 33:18)
Paul: Desire others to see the glory of God (Ephesians 1:18)
Solomon: Meditate often on the glory of God (2 Chronicles 6:13–7:3)
Jonathan Edwards: Proclaim the glory of God to others (*Ruth's Resolution*, Ruth 1:16)
The Psalmist: Confess your sin and walk in holiness as a response to His creation and His written Word (Psalm 19)

Table 3. REFLECT Method of Prayer - Step 2

EXAMINE YOUR MOTIVES & MANNER (STEP 2)
Ways & Words (Matthew 6:5-7)
Prayerlessness & Lust (James 4:1-4)
Impenetrable Ceilings (1 Peter 3:7)
Quiet & Peaceable life (1 Timothy 2:1–7)
Asking (Matthew 7:7-11)
Persevering (Luke 18:1-8)
Watching (Luke 21:34-36)

Table 4. REFLECT Method of Prayer - Step 3

FACE LIFE WITH SCRIPTURES (STEP 3)
Hannah   (1 Samuel 1:4-11. 1 Samuel 2:1-10)
Daniel   (Daniel 2:14-23)
Josiah   (2 Kings 22:8-20)
Information + Application = Sanctification   **Bible + Obedience = Godliness**
Thinking   (Philippians 4:8)
Doing   (Philippians 4:9)
Asking   (1 John 5:14)
Approaching   (Hebrews 4:15-16)
Helping   (1 Corinthians 10:13)

Table 5. REFLECT Method of Prayer - Step 4

LOVING GOD AND LOVING PEOPLE (STEP 4)
Defining Love   (1 Corinthians 13:1-8)
Loving Truth   (Psalm 119:97, 113, 163)
Loving Sacrificially   (Romans 5:6–11)
Without humility, there is no reconciliation   (Philippians 2:5-11)
First Love   (Revelation 2:1-7)
Test: Loving Others   (1 John 3:17–18)

Table 6. REFLECT Method of Prayer - Step 5

EXPECT SUFFERING & PERSECUTION (STEP 5)
Stephen   (Acts 7:54-60)
Paul   (2 Cor. 11:22-32)
Job   (Job 1:13-2:10)
Daniel's Three Friends   (Daniel 3:12-30)
Nehemiah   (Nehemiah 1:11-2:8)
Paul & Silas   (Acts 16:22-40)
Jesus Christ   (Matthew 26:36-44)

Table 7. REFLECT Method of Prayer - Step 6

CONCERN YOURSELF WITH THE KINGDOM (STEP 6)
Life, Death, and Judgment (Hebrews 9:27)
Authority & the Authorized Message (Matthew 28:16-20)
Kingdom's Work - Praying for Open Doors (Colossians 4:3, Ephesians 6:19)
Kingdom's Workers - Praying for Help (Matthew 9:38, 2 Thessalonians 3:1-2, John 17:9-20)
Kingdom's Wayward - Praying for Unbelievers (Matthew 5:44-48, Jude 1:20-25)

Table 8. REFLECT Method of Prayer - Step 7

TAKE EVERY OPPORTUNITY (STEP 7)
Be Diligent (2 Peter 1:5-11)
Remember Christ's Death, Burial, and Resurrection (1 Corinthians 15:1-4)
Remember God's Forgiveness (2 Corinthians 5:21, Colossians 2:13-14)
Be Thankful (1 Thessalonians 5:18)
Think Rightly (Philippians 4:8)
Be Pure & Holy (1 John 3:3, 1 Peter 1:14-16)
Bear Fruit for the Lord (Colossians 1:10)
Be a Wise Steward (1 Peter 4:10)
Beware of the Devil's Tactics (1 John 2:16)
Persevere in Trials (James 1:12, James 5:11)
Remember Your Time is Short & Limited (James 4:14)
Remember Our Future Judgment (2 Corinthians 5:10)
Hope in Christ (1 Peter 1:13)
Be Diligent (2 Peter 1:5-11)

Before you get overwhelmed by so much information, remember this is simply a guide for your prayers. As you study and read these texts, look for opportunities in the Scriptures to apply these truths. This approach will help you regain sharpness and focus on prayer as you engage the world in your walk in this world. As ambassadors for Christ, may your prayers REFLECT the glory of God!

INSTRUCTION

You are probably very familiar with the three basic steps of Bible study:

- Observation: understanding what the passage says.
- **Interpretation:** understanding what the passage means.
- **Application:** understanding how to apply the passage.

Let's begin with observation. There are three kinds of observations we need to complete at this stage: (1) 5Ws

& 1H, (2) Theological, and (3) Relational. This stage of observation is only preliminary for the purpose of prayer. We will go much deeper into our Biblical text analysis in future steps. Let's begin with the first type of observation, the 5Ws, and 1H.

Observing Inductively (5Ws & 1H)

Asking questions is one of the most basic approaches to discovering the truth. But one must ask the right questions. The foundational questions for Bible study are as follows: who, what, when, where, why, and how. For additional questions, see the Socratic Method of Questioning downloadable document: http://courses.cs.vt.edu/cs2104/Summer13/Notes/SocraticQ.pdf.

Now, there are many more questions about the Biblical text. For example, word study questions, grammar questions, historical background, theological background, and cross-checking are some of the initial questions for studying the Bible. We will examine more questions in the chapters to come. Remember, a deeper study is only possible by penetrating questions and illumination by the Spirit.

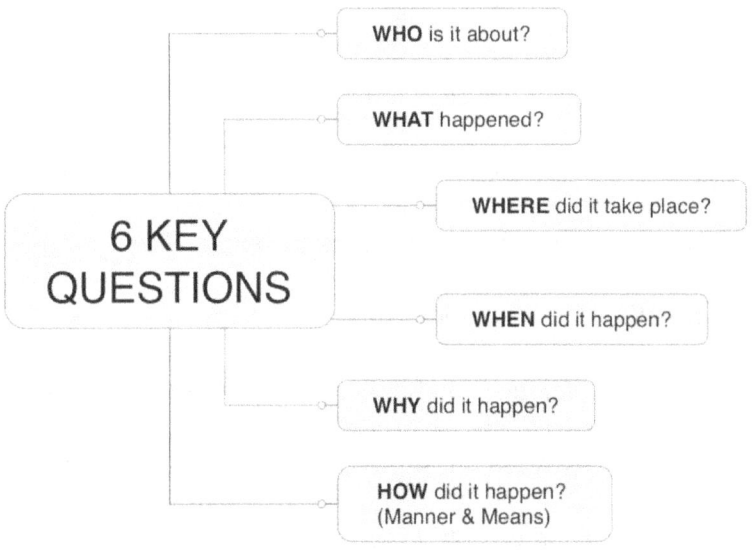

Figure 1. Six Key Questions

As you read and observe the text on your first reading through the text, write down or type the questions that first come to mind in your notes. If the Biblical text answers the questions, note the answer. However, if you don't have an answer to a question, then write down the question. This step is so important. **Don't neglect**

this step! These questions will remind you what to study later. Furthermore, adding these questions to your sermon at strategic locations can help re-engage the audience.

Part of human nature is to be curious. So, more than likely, your audience will ask themselves these very same questions when they hear the Biblical text for the first time. This strategy is a fantastic way to connect with the audience and help them avoid being distracted from unanswered questions echoing in their heads as you teach and preach. I recommend placing these questions right before an explanation of the passage. At the end of this section, I will provide Old and New Testament examples to demonstrate this technique. Let's proceed by observing theologically.

Observing Theologically
The second type of early observation is theological. As you read through the Biblical text again, you will be

asking if the text touches upon a theological theme. Table 9 lists all the major theological themes. It's important to remember that at this stage, you are simply writing down the theological theme of the verse. If you think the passage contributes additional insight, note the verse, the theme, and the fundamental idea. Some passages have more than one theological theme, but most have at least one primary theme. Later in the study, you will confirm this information and identify the most significant and predominant theological themes. Integrating theology into your sermon is the best way to add depth to your message. We'll provide an Old Testament example and a New Testament example at the end of this section.

Table 9. Theological Themes

13 THEOLOGICAL THEMES	
01 Bibliology / The Bible	08 Anthropology / Man
02 Theology / God the Father	09 Hamartiology / Sin
03 Christology / God the Son	10 Soteriology / Salvation
04 Pneumatology / God the Spirit	11 Israelology / Israel
05 Cosmology / Spiritual & Material World	12 Ecclesiology / The Church
06 Angelology / Angels	13 Eschatology / Future
07 Demonology / Satan and Demons	

Observing Relationally

The third type of observation is relational. Here, we will look at the text and see how this affects our vertical relationship with God and our horizontal relationships with believers and unbelievers. Besides praying over the 5Ws & 1H questions and the theological insights you might glean from studying the passage, you must humbly ask God to illuminate and providentially guide your studies. You need to incorporate prayer while you study.

As you examine the Scriptures, confess sin where your thinking, speaking, and doing are out of alignment with the Biblical text. This approach is where you begin to apply the text to your life and potentially to those you teach. Think of individuals in your congregation or Bible study who need to understand and apply these truths. Jot down their names in your notes and pray for them individually as you study the Scriptures. You will still need to study more in-depth to ensure the application is correct, but this is the first step in listening to the Spirit through the Scriptures.

By allowing God's Word to speak into your life, you will keep your heart from hardening to God's word and have a sensitivity to confess and repent of sin. The table below lists prayer categories to remember as you pray and study.

Table 10. Prayer Categories

PRAYER CATEGORIES	
01 Family	07 Ministries
02 Local church	08 Government (Local/National)
03 Co-Workers	09 Community
04 Friends	10 Countries
05 Extended Family	11 Recent Events
06 Missionaries	12 Personal

By now, you probably have noticed that these three types of observations do not require a computer. This approach is by design. This first step is to be relaxed and relational with you, the Scriptures, and God. I want you to be worshipful, thoughtful, and delight in knowing God and obeying His Word. It is too easy to jump on the proverbial "treadmill" and run the race toward the finishing message, never pausing for intense meditation, feeding your soul, and communing with God our Father. Your best teaching will occur when you experience spiritual rest and refreshment through illumination and transformation and encounter the Living God in His living Word. This prayer time must take place before you open your mouth to speak to others. Therefore, start, saturate, and secure your studies with an intimate prayer time.

APPLICATION

To help you become effective in observing the text, I have included two example passages: one from Psalm 103:1-5 and one from Matthew 8:23-27.

Old Testament: Psalm 103:1–5 (NASB95)

1 Bless the LORD, O my soul, And all that is within me, bless His holy name. **2** Bless the LORD, O my soul, And forget none of His benefits; **3** Who pardons all your iniquities, Who heals all your diseases; **4** Who redeems your life from the pit, Who crowns you with lovingkindness and compassion; **5** Who satisfies your years with good things, So that your youth is renewed like the eagle.

Table 11. Old Testament Observation Exercise

	VERSE	5Ws & 1H	THEOLOGY
1	Bless the Lord, O my soul, And all that is within me, His holy name.	**Why** does the passage begin with "Bless"? **Why** is the soul involved? **What** is the soul? **What** is "all that is within me"? **What** are the implications of God's name being holy?	Theology (God) Anthropology (Man)
Prayer	Why don't I bless the Lord when I begin to pray? Forgive me, Father, when I pray. Help me not be distracted. Help me to give You all my attention.		

Table 11. (continued)

	VERSE	5Ws & 1H	THEOLOGY
2	Bless the Lord, O my soul, And forget none of His benefits	**Why** is Bless repeated? **Why** is Soul repeated? **Why** should we not forget his benefits? Do we forget?	Theology Anthropology
Prayer	I confess that sometimes I forget Your blessings!		
3	Who pardons all your iniquities, Who heals all your diseases;	**How** does God pardon all iniquities? **What** types of diseases, since believers still get sick?	Theology Anthropology Hamartiology Eschatology
Prayer	I am so thankful for the complete forgiveness of all my past, present, and future sins!		

Table 11. (continued)

	VERSE	5Ws & 1H	THEOLOGY
4	Who redeems your life from the pit, Who crowns you with loving kindness and compassion;	**When** does the redemption happen? **What** is the pit? **What** does crown signify?	Theology Anthropology Hamartiology Eschatology
Prayer	I praise you, Father, for your kindness and compassion shown through Jesus Christ, my Lord, and Savior!		
5	Who satisfies your years with good things, So that your youth is renewed like the eagle	**What** kind of satisfaction? **How** are we renewed like an eagle?	Theology Anthropology
Prayer	Help me, Father, to be satisfied in You and the good things from your hand.		

NOTE: This is not an exhaustive list of observations, but it will help guide you in your observations.

New Testament: Matthew 8:23–27 (NASB95)

23 When He got into the boat, His disciples followed Him. **24** And behold, there arose a great storm on the sea, so that the boat was being covered with the waves; but Jesus Himself was asleep. **25** And they came to Him and woke Him, saying, "Save us, Lord; we are perishing!" **26** He said to them, "Why are you afraid, you men of little faith?" Then He got up and rebuked the winds and the sea, and it became perfectly calm. **27** The men were amazed, and said, "What kind of a man is this, that even the winds and the sea obey Him?"

NOTE: This event appears in Mark 4:35-41 and Luke 8:22-35. Therefore, you should align these three texts to understand the order of events and details. Below is my ordering of events. Please remember that the following arrangement came after I completed my word studies. However, I am providing this example as a guide should you want to attempt to order the texts for yourself. Some passages repeat since they combine two or more events into one verse.

Scene 1 - Getting into the Boat

- Mark 4:35 On that day, when evening came, He said to them, "Let us go over to the other side."

- Mark 4:36 Leaving the crowd, they took Him along with them in the boat, just as He was; and other boats were with Him.

- Matthew 8:23 When He got into the boat, His disciples followed Him.

- Luke 8:22 Now on one of those days Jesus and His disciples got into a boat, and He said to them, "Let us go over to the other side of the lake." So they launched out.

Scene 2 - The Storm Arose

- Mark 4:37 And there arose a fierce gale of wind, and the waves were breaking over the boat so much that the boat was already filling up.

Scene 3 - The Storm Descends, and Jesus Begins to Sleep

- Luke 8:23 But as they were sailing along He fell

asleep; and a fierce gale of wind descended on the lake, and they began to be swamped and to be in danger.

Scene 4 - The Storm is on the Sea

- Matthew 8:24 And behold, there arose a great storm on the sea, so that the boat was being covered with the waves; but Jesus Himself was asleep.

Scene 5 - Water Hits the Boat and Jesus is Asleep

- Matthew 8:24 And behold, there arose a great storm on the sea, so that the boat was being covered with the waves; but Jesus Himself was asleep.

Scene 6 - The Boat Fills with Water and Jesus Sleeps

- Mark 4:37 And there arose a fierce gale of wind, and the waves were breaking over the boat so much that the boat was already filling up.

- Luke 8:23 But as they were sailing along He fell asleep; and a fierce gale of wind descended on the lake, and they began to be swamped and to be in danger.

Scene 7 - *Waking Jesus & Sensing Doom*

- Mark 4:38 Jesus Himself was in the stern, asleep on the cushion; and they woke Him and said to Him, "Teacher, do You not care that we are perishing?"
- Luke 8:24 They came to Jesus and woke Him up, saying, "Master, Master, we are perishing!" And He got up and rebuked the wind and the surging waves, and they stopped, and it became calm.
- Matthew 8:25 And they came to Him and woke Him, saying, "Save us, Lord; we are perishing!"

Scene 8 - *Confronting Unbelief the First Time*

- Matthew 8:26 He said to them, "Why are you afraid, you men of little faith?" Then He got up and rebuked the winds and the sea, and it became perfectly calm.

Scene 9 - Calming the Storm

- Luke 8:24 They came to Jesus and woke Him up, saying, "Master, Master, we are perishing!" And He got up and rebuked the wind and the surging waves, and they stopped, and it became calm.

- Matthew 8:26 He said to them, "Why are you afraid, you men of little faith?" Then He got up and rebuked the winds and the sea, and it became perfectly calm.

- Mark 4:39 And He got up and rebuked the wind and said to the sea, "Hush, be still." And the wind died down and it became perfectly calm.

Scene 10 - Confronting Unbelief the Second Time

- Luke 8:25 And He said to them, "Where is your faith?" They were fearful and amazed, saying to one another, "Who then is this, that He commands even the winds and the water, and they obey Him?"

- Mark 4:40 And He said to them, "Why are you afraid? How is it that you have no faith?"

Scene 11 - Questioning the Identity of Jesus

- Matthew 8:27 The men were amazed, and said, "What kind of a man is this, that even the winds and the sea obey Him?"
- Luke 8:25 And He said to them, "Where is your faith?" They were fearful and amazed, saying to one another, "Who then is this, that He commands even the winds and the water, and they obey Him?"
- Mark 4:41 They became very much afraid and said to one another, "Who then is this, that even the wind and the sea obey Him?"

Table 12. New Testament Observation Exercise

	VERSE	5Ws & 1H	THEOLOGY
23	When He got into the boat, His disciples followed Him.	**What** events took place before Jesus got into the boat? **Where** did they come from and **where** are they going? **What** kind of boat? **Who** are the disciples getting into the boat? **Why** are the disciples following Jesus?	Christology (Christ) Anthropology (Man)
Prayer	Help me to follow Jesus.		

Table 12. (continued)

VERSE	5Ws & 1H	THEOLOGY
24 And behold, there arose a great storm on the sea, so that the boat was being covered with the waves; but Jesus Himself was asleep.	**What** is the purpose of this storm? **How** much water was coming into the boats? **Why** is Jesus sleeping?	Christology Cosmology
Prayer	Help me to understand the purpose of this storm and Christ's tiredness.	

Table 12. (continued)

	VERSE	5Ws & 1H	THEOLOGY
25	And they came to Him and woke Him, saying, "Save us, Lord; we are perishing!"	**How** terrible was this storm? **Why** were these fishermen thinking they were going to die?	Cosmology Anthropology Christology
Prayer	Would I be afraid in similar circumstances?		

Table 12. (continued)

	VERSE	5Ws & 1H	THEOLOGY
26	He said to them, "Why are you afraid, you men of little faith?" Then He got up and rebuked the winds and the sea, and it became perfectly calm.	**Why** did Jesus rebuke their fear and faith? **What** was missing in their faith? **How** was Jesus able to calm the storm so quickly?	Anthropology Hamartiology Christology Cosmology
Prayer	Help me, Father, to see areas where my faith is little.		

Table 12. (continued)

	VERSE	5Ws & 1H	THEOLOGY
27	The men were amazed, and said, "What kind of a man is this, that even the winds and the sea obey Him?"	**Why** were the men amazed? **Why** did they not understand that Jesus is God and can control the weather?	Anthropology Christology Cosmology
	Help me understand the identity and power of Christ correctly.		
	NOTE: This is not an exhaustive list, but to guide you in your observations.		

PRESENTATION

- https://www.DigitalSword.org/prayer
- Download the following worksheet to guide your Bible study.
- Review the training videos to help you integrate prayer and worship as you study with your computer.

SUMMARY

Goal

- Effectively worship God through the entire study-to-sermon process, seeking the illumination and transformation of yourself and those who will hear the message, calling individuals to be like Christ with the help of the Holy Spirit.

Strategy

- Prayerfully seek illumination and insight into the author's intended meaning from the Biblical text so that you and your audience can understand and apply the message correctly.

Tactics

- Establish a simple schedule to pray daily to God the Father through the Son with the help of the Holy Spirit.
- Read and pray through the Biblical text, writing down your questions and observations about the

text daily. Integrate a portion of these questions and answers into the sermon.

- Confess any sin revealed by the passage that comes to mind and turn away from evil with the Lord's help.
- Ask God to correct your thinking and help you change all behaviors that contradict the Biblical text's true meaning and application.
- Memorize and practice recalling the Biblical passage.
- Before the preaching event, ask God for specific opportunities to apply the text to your life.
- Ask God to reveal the Biblical text that has been lived out by others in the past or present in the body of Christ.
- Ask God to help the audience understand and apply the message to their lives.
- Ask God to help you persevere through the change process until you understand the

passage.

- Begin writing down some initial thoughts for the opening and closing prayer of the sermon.
- At the end of the study process, integrate the key questions and observations into your sermon so your audience can easily engage with the Biblical text.

Pitfalls & Warnings

- The number one pitfall is not to pray. Therefore, start with an amount of prayer time you can manage throughout the week. Do not incrementally increase your prayer time until you have prayed for the same amount of time for seven consecutive days.
- Always write down your questions and observations upon the initial reading of the Biblical text. These are essential for the message and help you connect to your audience more effectively. Remember, when you read the text

for the first time, all sorts of questions come to mind, but by the end of the studying process, you have answered those questions and might not even be able to recall those original questions. However, your audience has not studied the text, and these questions will form in their mind, distracting them from listening to you and your sermon. Therefore, you will truly connect with the audience by integrating these questions and observations from your prayer journal into your message.

- Hypocrisy, hard-heartedness, pride, and laziness are the greatest enemies of a transformed life. Effort yourself to be a holy and obedient preacher, and do not hesitate to repent when the Biblical text confronts you with the need for personal and immediate change. Get on your knees if necessary!

EXCEL STILL MORE

- Was there praying before the sermon, and did the prayer reflect the message of the Biblical text to be preached?
- Was there a prayer that followed the sermon, and did the prayer reflect the message of the Biblical text?
- Was the prayer centered on God, rooted in the Biblical text, and reflective of the Biblical text?
- Did the prayer direct the congregation to worship God and encourage them to obey the Biblical text?
- What elements of the acronym REFLECT were in the prayers?
- Did the sermon integrate the initial observations and questions you noted when reading the Biblical text?

RECOMMENDED BOOKS

- Boa, Kenneth. *Handbook to Prayer: Praying*

Scripture back to God. Atlanta: Trinity House, 1993.

- Bounds, Edward M. *Power through Prayer.* Chicago: Moody, 2009.

- Fallahee, John. *REFLECT the Glory of God in Prayer.* Milwaukee, WI: DigitalSword, 2019.

- MacArthur, John F., Jr. *Alone with God.* MacArthur Study Series. Wheaton, IL: Victor Books, 1995.

- Müller, George. *Autobiography of George Müller: A Million and a Half in Answer to Prayer.* London: J. Nisbet and Co., 1914.

- Piper, John. *A Hunger for God: Desiring God through Fasting and Prayer.* Wheaton, IL: Crossway Books, 1997.

- Rosscup, James E. *An Exposition on Prayer in the Bible.* Bellingham, WA: Lexham Press, 2008.

DIGITAL SWORD

CHAPTER TWO

FINDING THE TREASURE IN THE TEXT

"The entrance of thy words giveth light; It giveth understanding unto the simple."

— The Psalmist, Psalm 119:130

PURPOSE

Learn to discover the author's point of the passage at the beginning of the study process.

PREPARATION

It is Sunday morning, and the teacher or preacher announces the passage; together, you read the Biblical text and then look at the preacher's outline. Your initial thoughts, "this looks interesting," and you ready yourself for the preaching journey. But by the time the sermon is over, you look back at the outline, scratch your head, and say, "I just don't see the connection between the sermon, the Biblical text, and the outline." It seemed there were two destinations, one for the preacher and one for the Bible. Although the terrain looked similar at times, in the end, the sermon's point was not the point of the Biblical text. Has this been your experience on a Sunday morning, spiritual retreat, or a Christian conference? How does this happen? Is it possible to have two different routes to the same destination?

The problem I am exposing occurs all too often among preachers. Their outline does not follow nor flow from the Biblical text. That is why you see two different routes and two different destinations. This kind of failure is genuinely tragic.

I believe this is one of the most significant hindrances to effective preaching. Too many preachers hijack the author's intended message, superimpose their message, and obscure God's message for their own. On more occasions than one can count, we have sat through more than one sermon that does not reflect the Holy Spirit's point. When this happens, there is confusion, lack of clarity, and undermining of God's authority. It can happen because a text is difficult to understand.

However, it can also occur due to a lack of preparation. The underlying cause may be a lack of discipleship and training. Sadly, it may even result from a desire to tickle ears and please the audience rather than please God. You might be wondering how one can study the Bible and deliver an engaging message that reflects God's intended meaning and avoids missing the point of the passage.

This issue is personal for me and may even be for you. When I first began teaching and preaching, one of my biggest struggles was determining the point of the passage. All too often, I would research the Scriptures, believing I understood the primary point, only to discover that I had missed the mark at the end of the study process. With little time left, I would have to return to my sermon and fix the flaws.

It was so frustrating, time-consuming, and undermined my confidence. Do you have such a struggle? If so, you are not alone. It is a genuine issue for anyone teaching and preaching. To miss the point of the passage is a failure to understand God, which will never end well for you or your listeners. King David reveals the importance of knowing and obeying God's Word in Psalm 19:10-11 "They are more desirable than gold, yes than much fine gold; Sweeter also than honey and the drippings of the honeycomb. Moreover, by them, Your servant is warned; In keeping them, there is great reward." Applying a wrongly interpreted passage may result in sin and a loss of reward.

So, how do we find the treasure in the text? How do we find and outline the major and minor points of the passage and ensure we are truly hearing what God has to say in the Scriptures? How do we discover the point of the passage at the 'front end' rather than at the 'back end' before time runs out and it is time to teach and preach?

INSTRUCTION

Let me introduce a process that I have been using since 2008, which has significantly guided my studies and helped me find the point of the passage more quickly and easily. But before we proceed, I must put forth a disclaimer. There are many methods and approaches to accomplish this step. Each one has its merits and can achieve the same goal. For example, phrasing, grammatical diagramming, block diagramming, structuring, and arcing to name a few.

Unfortunately, many of these approaches are time-consuming and require a thorough knowledge of Hebrew and Greek grammar, a significant barrier for most individuals. We need a resource that is accurate to the original language and grammar of the Bible but is easy to follow along and use. Fortunately, such resources exist, of which two stand out:

Old Testament:
Andersen, Francis I., and A. Dean Forbes. *The Hebrew Bible: Andersen-Forbes Phrase Marker Analysis*. Bellingham, WA: Logos Bible Software, 2009.

New Testament
Porter, Stanley E., Matthew Brook O'Donnell, Jeffrey T. Reed, and Randall Tan, OpenText.org. *The OpenText.org Syntactically Analyzed Greek New Testament: Clause Analysis*; OpenText.org Clause Analysis. Logos Bible Software, 2006.

APPLICATION

These resources were only available in Logos Bible Software when this book was published. Let me show you how to use these resources to outline any passage quickly, easily, and accurately, beginning with a New Testament example and then followed by an Old

Testament example.

New Testament Example: Matthew 8:23-27
(Utilizing OpenText Clause Analysis)

Step 1 – Learn seven abbreviations

The following list represents the key abbreviations you need to know and memorize when using the *OpenText* resource.

1. PC – Primary Clause | Main Idea
2. **EC – Embedded Clause** | Supports and further explains the primary clause/phrase
3. **SC – Secondary Clause** | Supports and further explains the primary clause/phrase
4. **P – Predicator/Verb** | This is the action of the clause/phrase
5. **S – Subject** | This is the subject of the clause/phrase
6. **C – Complement** | Completes the predicator/verb. Answers the questions: who or what

DIGITAL SWORD

7. **A – Adjunct** | Modifies the predicator/verb, adding additional information. Answers the questions: where, when, why, or how.

Step 2 – Learn to follow the lines
In Figure 2, you can see an excerpt from Matthew 8:23 from the *OpenText* resource used to outline the New Testament. The word order follows the original Greek language but uses a different English translation. Therefore, it will not read like your favorite English Bible.

A. Find the Line Divisions
Look for the horizontal lines In Figure 2. Locate #1 and #2. These lines identify where the clause begins (#1) and ends (#2).

B. Find the PC
The next step in reading this line graph is to locate the PC (see #3 in Figure 2) between these line divisions. The PC represents the primary clause. Our example below starts with the words "followed" and extends down to the word "his." This PC is the primary clause, the main idea. A Bible verse can have one or more

64

primary clauses, and a clause can extend across multiple verses.

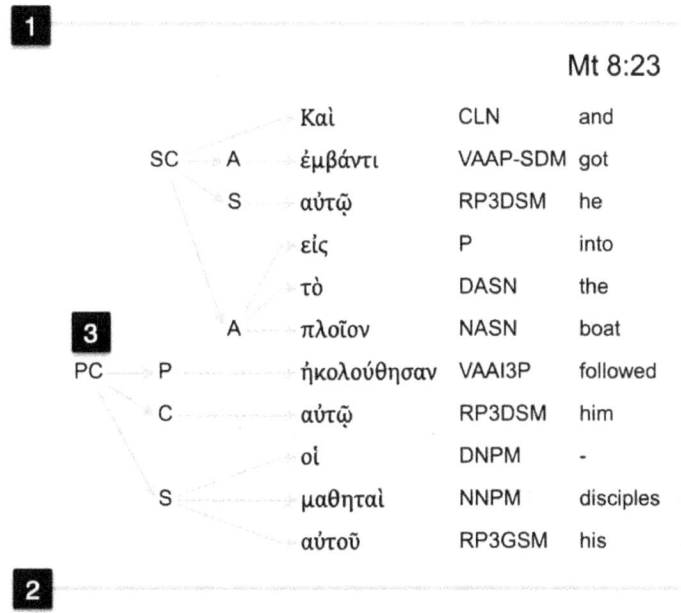

Figure 2. Primary Clause

As you can see, *OpenText* and Logos Bible Software make it easy to identify the primary clause, which contains the major points of the passage.

Step 3 – Locate the subject and verb of the primary clause

Nearly every primary clause (PC) has a subject and a verb. Of course, there are always exceptions, but even when the subject is absent, the context will inform you, removing any guesswork.

A. Verb

Find the 'P.' In Figure 3 below, locate the P (Predicator/Verb) directly flowing from the PC. It is noted by #1. It is the main verb of the main clause of the main point. Our main verb is "followed."

B. Subject

Find the 'S.' In the example below, locate the S (Subject) directly flowing from the PC. It is noted by #2. It is the main subject of the main clause. Our main subject is "disciples his" or "His disciples."

```
                                              Mt 8:23
                    Καὶ              CLN        and
        SC    A     ἐμβάντι          VAAP-SDM   got
              S     αὐτῷ             RP3DSM     he
                    εἰς              P          into
                    τὸ               DASN       the
        [1]   A     πλοῖον           NASN       boat
PC      P           ἠκολούθησαν      VAAI3P     followed
        C           αὐτῷ             RP3DSM     him
                    οἱ               DNPM       -
        S           μαθηταὶ          NNPM       disciples
        [2]         αὐτοῦ            RP3GSM     his
```

Figure 3. Subject and Verb

NOTE: Sometimes, the subject and the verb are together. For example, in Matthew 8:24 of Figure 4, the subject "I" is paired with the verb "behold."

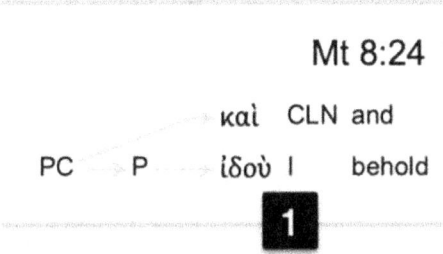

Figure 4. Verb with Paired Subject

C. Write it out

At this juncture, we must write or type out the subject and verb together to see the main idea and begin building our preliminary outline for teaching and preaching. For this example, we would write, "His disciples followed." Feel free to borrow the words and phrases from your preferred English translation.

Step 4 – Repeat this process for all remaining passages

Admittedly, I chose an easy passage to help you see that this procedure is not complex. Although there are more difficult passages, this process can work with any passage, and over time and with practice, you will handle those just as quickly. I recommend focusing solely on the primary clause on your first pass through the text. Remember to write these out, numbering your points as you go. Below is an example of a preliminary outline of the primary clauses with their subject and verbs for Matthew 8:23-27.

FINDING THE TREASURE IN THE TEXT

Preliminary Outline

1. His disciples followed **(Matthew 8:23)**

2. Behold **(Matthew 8:24)**

3. A great storm arose

4. Jesus was asleep

5. They (disciples) awoke (Jesus) **(Matthew 8:25)**

6. Lord save us

7. We are perishing

8. Jesus said **(Matthew 8:26)**

9. Little faith, are you?

10. (Jesus) rebuked

11. There was a great calm

12. Men were amazed **(Matthew 8:27)**

13. (What sort of man) This is?

You can see the main idea with the primary clauses discovered and written down. As they say, "Easy peasy!" Here is the treasure in the text! And you found it right away rather than at the end of some grueling, complex, uncertain, time-consuming process.

DIGITAL SWORD

Step 5 – Locate the secondary and embedded clauses with their subjects and verbs

Next, we need to identify the supporting ideas. Let us now look at the secondary and embedded clauses. Matthew 8:23 is in Figure 5 below.

```
                                              Mt 8:23
                     Καὶ           CLN        and
   [1] SC    A       ἐμβάντι       VAAP-SDM   got
             S       αὐτῷ          RP3DSM     he
            [2]      εἰς           P          into
                     τὸ            DASN       the
             A       πλοῖον        NASN       boat
PC      P            ἠκολούθησαν   VAAI3P     followed
        C            αὐτῷ          RP3DSM     him
                     οἱ            DNPM       -
        S            μαθηταὶ       NNPM       disciples
                     αὐτοῦ         RP3GSM     his
```

Figure 5. Secondary Clause with the Subject.

The secondary clause (SC) (#1) includes a subject (S) (#2). There is a verb ("got"), but interestingly, it functions adverbially and is labeled as an adjunct (A).

With this information, we will continue to update our preliminary outline.

1. His disciples followed (**Matthew 8:23**)
    a. He (Jesus) got into the boat

In this example, the author Matthew reveals the main point about the disciples following Jesus rather than Jesus getting into the boat!

Let's continue with Matthew 8:24. There are three primary clauses (see Figure 6). The second primary clause (PC) is the "great storm that arose." The secondary clause (SC) noted by #1 with the subject (S) "boat" and the verb (P) "was being inundated."

DIGITAL SWORD

```
                                        Mt 8:24
                            καὶ      CLN  and
                   PC   P   ἰδοὺ  I       behold

     PC   S       σεισμὸς      NNSM   storm
                  μέγας        JNSM   a great
          P       ἐγένετο      VAMI3S arose
                  ἐν           P      on
                  τῇ           DDSF   the
          A       θαλάσσῃ      NDSF   sea
                  ὥστε         CAR    so that
                  τὸ           DASN   the
  1  SC   S       πλοῖον       NASN   boat
          P       καλύπτεσθαι  VPPN   was being inundated
                  ὑπὸ          P      by
                  τῶν          DGPN   the
          A       κυμάτων      NGPN   waves

     PC   S       αὐτὸς        RP3NSMP he himself
                  δὲ           CLC    but
          P       ἐκάθευδεν    VIAI3S was asleep
```

Figure 6. Secondary Clause

Let us update our outline.

1. Behold (Matthew 8:24)

2. Great storm arose

   a. The boat was being inundated

3. Jesus was asleep

Matthew emphasizes how "the great storm arose" but

72

FINDING THE TREASURE IN THE TEXT

provides additional insight into how the storm began to cover the boat with water. Go ahead and identify the remaining secondary and embedded clauses and update your outline. When you have completed this step for Matthew 8:23-27, please compare it to my revised outline below.

1. His disciples followed (**Matthew 8:23**)

   a. He (Jesus) got into the boat

2. Behold (Matthew 8:24)

3. Great storm arose

   a. The boat was being inundated

4. Jesus was asleep

5. They (disciples) awoke (Jesus) (**Matthew 8:25**)

   a. Came

   b. Saying

6. Lord save us

7. We are perishing

8. Jesus said (**Matthew 8:26**)

9. Little faith, are you?

10. (Jesus) rebuked

       a. He (Jesus) got up
- 11. There was a great calm
- 12. Men were amazed (**Matthew 8:27**)
   - **a.** Saying
- 13. (What sort of man) This is?
   - **a.** Even the wind and the sea obey

By identifying the primary clauses with the subordinate secondary clauses and writing them down as a simple outline, you can rightly emphasize the primary ideas in the Biblical text and support them with the secondary ideas. This proven approach is how we handle the text accurately, preach clearly, and glorify God. You can be confident in the effectiveness of this process.

Step 6 – Grouping the main ideas

After you have outlined all the primary and secondary clauses, you will have an extensive list of information. However, this outline is too long and too detailed for preaching and teaching. You understand that most individuals appreciate three to five points in a sermon. So, we aim to group the information with these limitations in mind. So how do we do this quickly?

At this stage, it is too soon to look at the grammar and determine from the original language how to divide up the text. Instead, I prefer to take a more straightforward approach, knowing that later, as we study more in-depth, we can revise our initial decisions. There are seven basic ways to group our preliminary outline: (1) conversation, (2) location, (3) subject/topic, (4) action/event, (5) time, (6) theology, and (7) arguments. There are undoubtedly many more ways to group, but these are the most common ones you will encounter.

Below is the list of primary and second clauses after completing the grouping process.

*The Preliminary Outline **After** Grouping by Change in Events*

I. Following Jesus into The Boat

    1. His disciples followed (**Matthew 8:23**)

        a. He (Jesus) got into the boat

II. The Great Storm Arose while Jesus Sleeps

    2. Behold (Matthew 8:24)

    3. Great storm arose

        a. The boat was being inundated

    4. Jesus was asleep

III. The Disciples Awoke Jesus Fearing for their Lives

    5. They (disciples) awoke (Jesus) (**Matthew 8:25**)

        a. Came

        b. Saying

    6. Lord save us

    7. We are perishing

IV. Jesus Questioned Lack of Faith & Rebuked Storm

    8. Jesus said (Matthew 8:26)

    9. Little faith, are you?

    10. (Jesus) rebuked

      a. He (Jesus) got up
  11. There was a great calm

V. The Disciples were amazed
  12. Men were amazed (**Matthew 8:27**)
      a. Saying
  13. (What sort of man) This is?
      a. Even the winds and the sea obey

As you can see, we could group the list of thirteen primary ideas into five ideas, well within our three to five preaching points. If your grouping is different than mine, that is OK. Remember, your outline is still preliminary and open to further refinement as we proceed with the Bible study and sermon preparation process.

If your selected passage requires more than three to five groups, you have two options. Reduce the number of passages preached for the sermon or combine the groupings. The first option allows you to preach more details from the text, but it will take longer to teach through it. The second option will result in preaching fewer details from the Bible. Either way, it is something for you to pray through and be sensitive to the Spirit's leading and your audience's needs. Too much detail can overwhelm, and too little detail can underwhelm.

If you are uncertain at this point, leave the more detailed outline in place, proceed with the Bible study process, and decide later. As you move through the Bible study process and learn more information from your research, you will be in a better position to determine the level of detail appropriate for your audience, given the amount of time allotted for your sermon.

Old Testament Example: Psalm 103
(Utilizing *Andersen-Forbes Phrase Marker Analysis*)

Step 1 – Learn three abbreviations
The following list represents the key abbreviations you need to know and memorize when using the *Andersen-Forbes Phrase Marker Analysis* resource.

- **CLOBLQ** – Individual Clause | Main Idea
- **VBGRAM** – Verb | This is the action of the clause/phrase
- **SBJGRAM** – Subject | This is the subject of the clause/phrase

Step 2 – Learn to follow the lines

Below, in Figure 7, you can see an excerpt of Psalm 103:1 from the *Andersen-Forbes Phrase Marker Analysis* resource used for outlining the Old Testament. The word order follows the original Hebrew language but uses a different English translation, so it will not read like your English Bible.

A. Find the line divisions

First, look for the horizontal lines. Look for #1 and #2 in Figure 7. These lines identify where the first clause begins (#1) and ends (#2).

DIGITAL SWORD

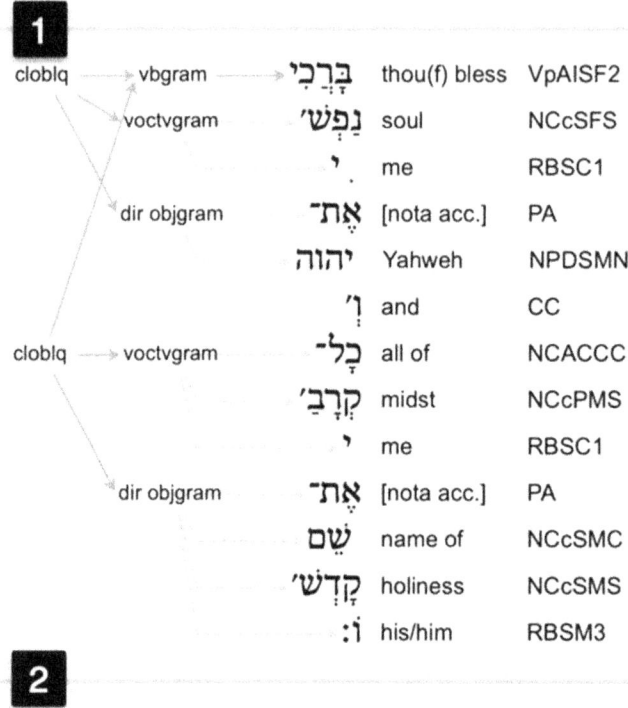

Figure 7. Clause

B. Find the cloblq

The next step in reading this line graph is to locate the *cloblq* between these line divisions. These are noted by #3 and #4 in Figure 8 below. The first clause (#3) and second clause (#4) are interesting because they share the same verb "blessed."

FINDING THE TREASURE IN THE TEXT

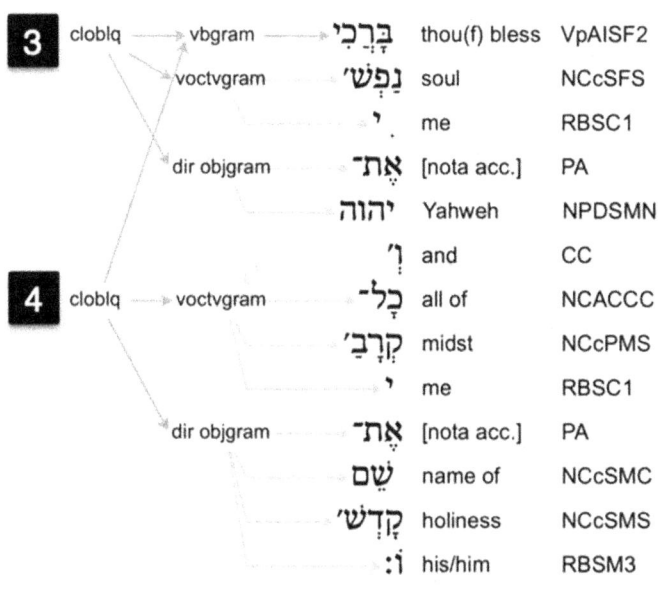

Figure 8. Clause

As you can see, and Logos Bible Software identify the clauses that contain the passage's primary points.

Step 3 – Locate the subject and verb of the clause
Like the Greek New Testament, nearly every clause has a subject and verb in the Hebrew Old Testament. As mentioned earlier, there are exceptions, but even when the subject is absent, the context will inform you, removing any guesswork.

A. Verb

Find the 'vbgram' in Psalm 103:1. In Figure 9 below, locate the 'vbgram' (Verb) that directly flows from the 'cloblq' (Clause). It is noted by #5. It is the main verb of the clause. Our verb is "bless" (#6).

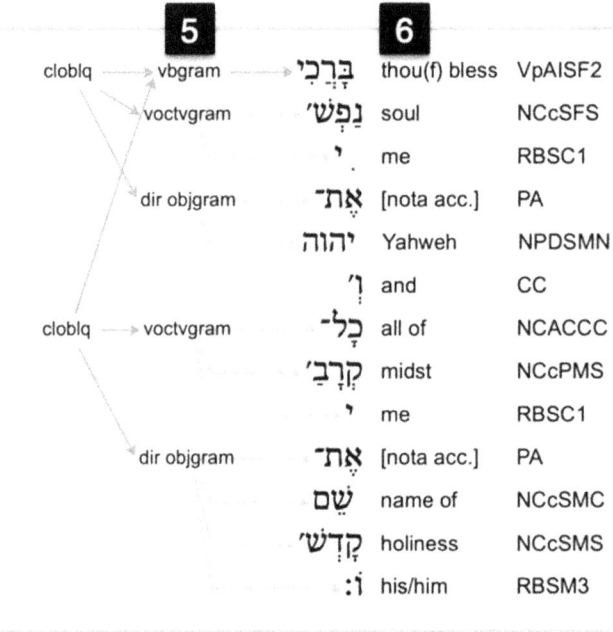

Figure 9. Verb and its paired subject

B. Subject

Find the 'sbjgram.' In the example above from Figure 9, you will note there is no 'sbjgram.' The subject is joined to the verb "bless." The subject is "thou" or "you" in modern English. Additionally, the 'voctvgram' informs the reader of who is being addressed. We can

FINDING THE TREASURE IN THE TEXT

include this information with the subject. At the end of Psalm 103:5 in Figure 10 below, it reveals the 'sbjgram' (#7) to be "youth thee" or "your youth" in modern English.

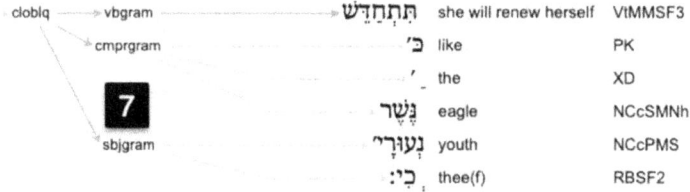

Figure 10. Subject

A. Write it Out

At this juncture, we need to write out the subject and verb together to see the main idea of the clause and begin building our preliminary outline for teaching and preaching. Psalm 103:1 preliminary outline:

1. You, my soul, bless (Yahweh) (**Psalm 103:1**)

2. All that is within me bless (His holy name)

Step 4 – Repeat this process for all remaining passages

The *Andersen-Forbes Phrase Marker Analysis* is much more challenging to read and use than the *OpenText*. Since Psalm 103 is twenty-two verses long, it will take some effort on your behalf to outline. However, we have provided below the preliminary outline for Psalm 103:1-5.

1. You, my soul, bless (Yahweh) **(Psalm 103:1)**
2. All that is within me bless (His holy name)
3. You, my soul, bless (Yahweh) **(Psalm 103:2a)**
4. One shall Not Forget (His benefits) **(Psalm 103:2b-5a)**
5. One is renewed **(Psalm 103:5b)**

Step 5 – Locate the secondary and embedded clauses with their subjects and verbs

You can see the main idea more clearly with the clauses discovered and written down. As they say, "Piece of cake!" It is the treasure in the text! And you found it almost as quickly as you did with the *OpenText* resource, but without some technical, challenging, and time-consuming process.

Next, we need to identify the supporting ideas. In Figure 11 below, you'll find Psalm 103:2-3. I have marked two secondary clauses (#1 & #3) and their main verbs (#2 &

#4). This step is challenging with *Andersen-Forbes Phrase Marker Analysis* since they are not marked as a secondary clause but rather flow in this example from the 'dir objgram' (Direct object) from the clause, which then flows from the 'cloblq' (Clause).

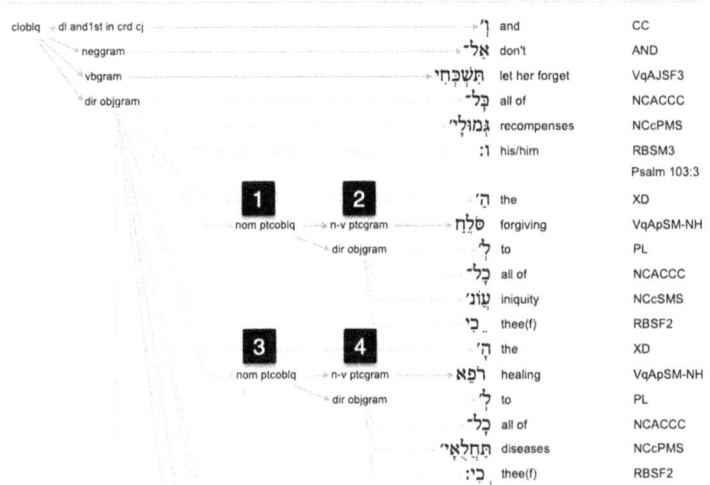

Figure 11. Secondary clauses

So, how do we outline this structure in Figure 11?

1. One shall Not Forget (His benefits) (**Psalm 103:2**)

    a. Forgiving (Psalm 103:3)

    b. Healing

As you can see, we have subordinated two of the five

benefits. The main idea is "one shall not forget." Go ahead and identify the remaining secondary clauses and update your outline. When you have completed this step for Psalm 103:1-5, please compare it to my revised outline below.

1. You, my soul, bless (Yahweh) (**Psalm 103:1**)
2. All that is within me bless (His holy name)
3. You, my soul, bless (Yahweh) (**Psalm 103:2**)
4. One shall Not Forget (His benefits)
   a. Forgiving (Psalm 103:3)
   b. Healing
   c. Redeeming (Psalm 103:4)
   d. Crowning
   e. Satisfying (Psalm 103:5)
   f. PURPOSE/RESULT: One is renewed

By identifying the primary clauses with the secondary clauses and writing both down as a simple outline, you will be in a better position to rightly emphasize the primary ideas in the Biblical text and support them with the secondary ideas. This process is how we handle the text accurately, preach clearly, and glorify God.

Step 6 – Grouping the main ideas

After identifying all the primary and secondary clauses, you need to group your list into three to five main ideas for teaching and preaching. As mentioned earlier, most individuals appreciate three to five points in a sermon, so we should attempt to group the information with these limitations in mind. If we had completed this exercise for all twenty-two verses, our list would have been extensive.

At this stage, it is too soon to look at the grammar and determine from the original language how to divide up the text. Instead, I prefer to take a more straightforward approach, knowing that later, as we study more in-depth, we can revise our initial decisions. Just like before, we will utilize the same seven basic ways to group our preliminary outline: (1) conversation, (2) location, (3) subject/topic, (4) action/event, (5) time, (6) theology, and (7) arguments. There are certainly many more ways to group, but these are the most common.

Below is the list of primary and second clauses after completing the grouping process.

The Preliminary Outline <u>After</u> Grouping by Change in Subject/Topic

I. Bless Yahweh
1. You, my soul, bless (Yahweh) (**Psalm 103:1**)
2. All that is within me bless (His holy name)
3. You, my soul, bless (Yahweh) (**Psalm 103:2a**)

II. Don't Forget Yahweh's Benefit
4. One shall Not Forget (His benefits) (**Psalm 103:2b**)
    a. Forgiving (Psalm 103:3)
    b. Healing
    c. Redeeming (Psalm 103:4)
    d. Crowning

e. Satisfying (Psalm 103:5)

   f. PURPOSE/RESULT: One is renewed

As you can see, we grouped the list of 4 primary ideas into two ideas, well within our three to five preaching points. If your grouping is different than mine, that is OK. Remember, this is still preliminary and open to further refinement as we proceed with the Bible study and sermon preparation process.

By the way, if your selected passage requires more than three to five groups, you have two options. Reduce the number of passages preached for the sermon or combine the groupings. The first option allows you to preach more details from the text, but it will take longer to teach through the various passages. The second option will result in preaching fewer details from the Bible. Either way, it is something for you to pray for and be sensitive to the Spirit's leading and your audience's needs. Too much detail can overwhelm, and too little detail can underwhelm.

If you are uncertain at this point, leave the more detailed outline in place, proceed with the Bible study process, and decide later. As you move through the Bible study process and learn more information from your research, you will be in a better position to determine the level of detail appropriate for your audience, given the amount of time allotted for your sermon.

Near the end of the chapter, be sure to check out the training videos for additional instruction. In my experience, one must outline somewhere between 10 to 15 passages to become comfortable with this process. But the effort is worth it! Nothing is more exciting than understanding God's Word and having the confidence to herald His truth precisely.

PRESENTATION

- https://www.DigitalSword.org/outline
- Download the following worksheet to guide your Bible study.
- Review the training videos to help you integrate prayer and worship as you study with your computer.

SUMMARY

Goal
- To produce an outline that reflects the Biblical text accurately.

Strategy
- Use the *OpenText* and *Andersen-Forbes Phrase Marker Analysis* to identify the primary and secondary clauses to create a preliminary outline for studying, teaching, and preaching.

Tactics
- Choose a passage for teaching and preaching
- Examine the syntactical diagram for your

passage and identify the primary and subordinate clauses with the main subject and main verb
- Create a preliminary outline from the biblical text with the syntactical diagram that you will be preaching
- Identify any other additional words you will be studying
- Add to your prayer journal any additional insights, observations, and unanswered questions
- Continue to pray through the text prescribed in the previous lesson

Pitfalls & Warnings
- The number one pitfall is to skip this step! Therefore, immediately after praying, review the videos if unsure of the process. Immediately begin working on the outline. It takes anywhere between 10-15 sessions to master this process.

Keep in mind some passages are more complex than others.

- Focus on the primary ideas in the text. Continue to write down the questions and observations as you outline the Biblical text. Note any additional insights you glean from reading and outlining the text.
- Keep in mind this step requires the accuracy of a scribe, requiring you to convert the visual syntactical diagram into a usable preaching/teaching outline.
- Do not proceed in the sermon process until you have completed this outline.

EXCEL STILL MORE

- Does the outline accurately follow the syntactical diagram, identifying the major and minor clauses?
- Were the main subjects and main verbs identified in the outline?

- Was the outline condensed into a digestible size of three to five points?
- Were the sub-points correctly identified and subordinated?

RECOMMENDED BOOKS

- Mounce, William D. *A Graded Reader of Biblical Greek:* Edited by Verlyn D. Verbrugge. Grand Rapids, MI: Zondervan, 1996.
- Kaiser, Walter C., Jr. *Toward an Exegetical Theology: Biblical Exegesis for Preaching and Teaching.* Grand Rapids, MI: Baker Academic, 1981.
- Richard, Ramesh. *Preparing Expository Sermons: A Seven-Step Method for Biblical Preaching.* Grand Rapids, MI: Baker Books, 2001.

CHAPTER THREE

REMOVING THE VEIL OF BABEL, PART 1

"Therefore is the name of it called Babel; because the LORD did there confound the language of all the earth: and from thence did the LORD scatter them abroad upon the face of all the earth."

— Moses the Prophet, Genesis 11:9

PURPOSE

Learn to work with the original languages of the Bible to gain deeper insights and handle the Word more accurately.

PREPARATION

A Jewish poet by the name of Haim Nachman Bialik stated, "Reading the Bible in translation is like kissing your new bride through a veil." I don't know about you, but on my wedding day, I did not want anything to get in the way of our first kiss as husband and wife. I wanted the full-orbed experience! Just as a veil can obscure the bride, our modern translation can obscure the author.

For you to experience the Word of God fully, to rightly divide Scriptures, and to study the Bible to understand the author's original meaning, you will need the ability to access the Old Testament Hebrew, occasionally Aramaic, and the New Testament Greek. However, if you do not have training in these languages, don't panic! Fortunately, even without formal education in these ancient languages, Bible software allows you to access word meanings and grammatical insights easily. Why is the original language so important? It has been my experience over the years that every debate or argument about the meaning of the Bible hinges on understanding the definition of a word in the original language and the corresponding grammar of the sentence. If you do not have any means to study the original language word meaning or grammar, then you will be incapable of evaluating the arguments and will be hindered from precisely understanding the Biblical text.

In an age of false teachers, competing narratives for the truth, and your personal growth in the Lord, it is critical you are fully equipped to take any and all steps to know what God's Word says and does not say in the original language. Unfortunately, this chapter will not make you a scholar or expert in the original languages. But you will be able to learn how to interact with Hebrew and Greek with Logos Bible Software.

INSTRUCTION

Learn the alphabet

Before we begin, may I offer helpful advice? Learn the Hebrew and Greek alphabets. Each language will take about 30 days to learn its letters and sounds. Logos Bible Software has a Hebrew and Greek Tutorial to assist you in this endeavor. You can also search the internet for video tutorials as well. Learning the letters and sounds will make Hebrew and Greek accessible. You will begin recognizing repeated words, especially those you look up in dictionaries often. Learning their definitions will take more time and effort, but your vocabulary and understanding will grow as you study more. For your convenience, I have included the Hebrew and Greek alphabet in the next several pages.

Table 13. Hebrew Alphabet

HEBREW ALPHABET			
Letter	Name	Sound	Our Alphabet
א	alef	silent	ʼ
ב	bet	b as in **b**ag	b
ג	gimel	g as in **g**irl	g
ד	daleth	d as in **d**ig	d
ה	he	h as in **h**elp	h
ו	waw	w as in **w**on	w
ז	zayin	z as in **z**ipper	z
ח	ḥet	ch as in ba**ch**	ḥ
ט	tet	t as in **t**ool	ṭ
י	yod	y as in **y**ellow	y
כ	kaf	k as in **k**ing	k
ל	lamed	l as in **l**ion	l
מ	mem	m as in **m**ore	m
נ	nun	n as in **n**ext	n
ס	samech	s as in **s**ell	s
ע	ʽayin	silent	ʽ
פ	pe	p as in **p**oor	p
צ	tsade	ts as in pi**ts**	ṣ
ק	qof	k as in **k**ite	q
ר	resh	r as in **r**ed	r
שׂ	sin	s as in **s**ip	ś
שׁ	shin	sh as in **sh**ore	š
ת	taw	t as in **t**ell	t

Table 14. Greek Alphabet

GREEK ALPHABET				
Upper	**Lower**	**Name**	**Sound**	**Our Alphabet**
ʽ	ʽ		h as in **h**ot	h
Α	α	alpha	a as in m**a**ma	a
Β	β	beta	b as in **b**ook	b
Γ	γ	gamma	g as in **g**o	g
Δ	δ	delta	d as in **d**one	d
Ε	ε	epsilon	e as in **e**gg	e
Ζ	ζ	zeta	z as in **z**eal dz as in mai**d**s	z
Η	η	eta	ē as in h**ey**	ē
Θ	θ	theta	th as in **th**anks	th
Ι	ι	iota	i as in k**i**t/i as in p**ee**k	y
Κ	κ	kappa	k as in **k**ick	k
Λ	λ	lambda	l as in **l**ove	l
Μ	μ	mu	m as in **m**ix	m
Ν	ν	nu	n as in **n**o	n
Ξ	ξ	xi	x as in bo**x**	x
Ο	ο	omicron	o as in l**o**t	o
Π	π	pi	p as in **p**lan	p
Ρ	ρ	rho	r as in **r**ed	r
Σ	σ, ς	sigma	s as in **s**ing	s
Τ	τ	tau	t as in **t**ough	t
Υ	υ	upsilon	u as in **ü**ber	u
Φ	φ	phi	ph as in **ph**oto	ph
Χ	χ	chi	ch as in sti**ck**y	ch
Ψ	ψ	psi	ps as in to**ps**	ps
Ω	ω	omega	o as in **o**h	ō

Word Study Basics

Studying the words in a Biblical passage is critical for understanding the meaning of the context. But where are you to begin? Let me overview the process I use for word studies. Then we will jump into some examples.

Step 1 – Start with Action: Verbs

If you recall, from chapter 2, we identified all the primary clauses and their verbs. We must begin with these verbs first. The verbs are so important and carry a lot of meaning to help you understand the context. Once you look up all these words, look up all the remaining verbs in the passage.

Step 2 – Focus on Other Key Words

A keyword is any word that, if removed from the sentence, would change the meaning of the sentence. Look at each word in the sentence. Observe how meaning would change when a particular keyword is removed from the sentence. As you grow your Hebrew and Greek vocabulary, you will look up fewer and fewer words.

Don't neglect this step and shortcut the process. Ultimately, putting in the hard work will save time, help you be more precise, and, most importantly, help you better understand the passage and the author's intended meaning.

Step 3 – Look up the definition: Meaning

Once you have identified the various words to look up, you must determine their meaning in their context. Dictionaries like Strong's and Vine's are a wonderful place to start. However, with Bible Software, you can take advantage of more scholarly resources that are more detailed and more precise. Keep in mind, without Bible software; these resources were only accessible to trained individuals who knew Hebrew and Greek. But this has all changed…you can study like a scholar! Before we move to the next section, remember context solely determines the meaning of any word! Words will have different shades of meaning depending on the other related words in the sentence. When you look up a dictionary definition, confirm the passage's specific contextual meaning by re-reading the sentence with the new definition in mind.

Step 4 – Look up its function: Morphology
This part of the word study process can be overwhelming. It requires a basic knowledge of grammar. However, the tools in Bible Software will simplify the process and help you gain grammatical insights, even if your knowledge is limited. This step aims to understand what the word is doing in the sentence. Here are some, but not all, the essential questions to ask when you begin to interact with words in a passage. In the next chapter, there will be a more significant discussion on grammar and morphology.

A. What kind of word is it?
Noun, verb, adjective, adverb, etc.

B. How does it function in the sentence?
Is it functioning as the subject, a direct object, an

indirect object, or further describing another word?

C. Is it a verb?

Is the action taking place in the past, present, or future? Who is doing the action? Who is receiving the action?

D. Is it singular or plural?

Plurality is not as apparent in English as in Hebrew and Greek. We might read 'you' in our English Bible, but is it singular or plural in the original language of Hebrew and Greek? Bible Software can help you answer this question quickly.

E. Is it related to another word in the sentence?

For example, an adjective modifying a noun, or adverb modifying a verb, or an article related to a noun.

Step 5 – Understand near and far contexts

As mentioned earlier, it is critical to understand the meaning of the word in its immediate context, the passage under examination. However, it may be necessary to expand your studies to understand the same word's meaning in other contexts, such as at the chapter or book level, or how other authors use the word in their contexts. See figure 12 for an understanding of the various circles of context.

Step 6 – Write out a definition in your own words
After you complete your research, it is essential to summarize what you have learned about each word. Your goal is to illustrate to others what each word means in its context to understand the author's intended meaning. Don't just provide definitions but rather engage the audience and help them see the value and applicability of these insights to their life.

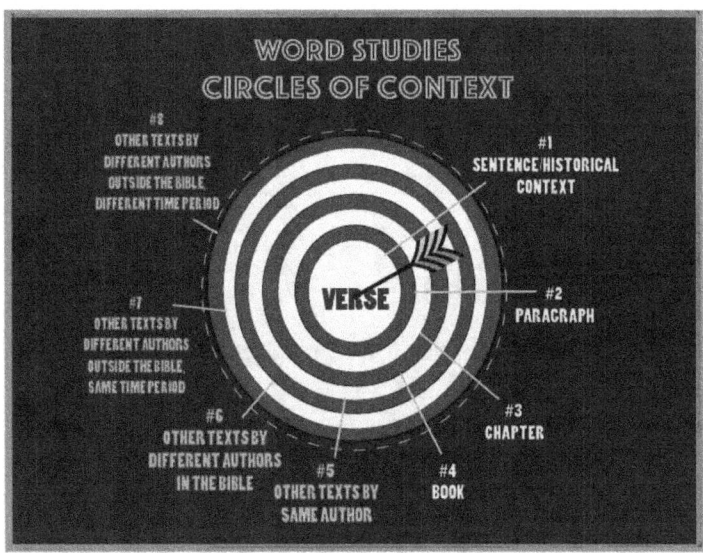

Figure 12. Circles of Context

APPLICATION

To improve your word study skills, we will look up the word 'disease' from Psalm 103:3 and the word 'asleep' from Matthew 8:24, as well as the parallel accounts in Mark 4:38 and Luke 8:23.

Psalm 103:3 - Disease

Step 1 – Start with Action: Verbs

There are many verbs to look up in Psalm 103:1-5. Using the six-step process, you should thoroughly analyze all the verbs and other significant keywords. However, our focus is on the word 'disease.' Therefore, proceed to Step 2.

Step 2 – Focus on Other Key Words

'Disease' is the second of five benefits the Psalmist lists from Psalm 103:3-5. God is the subject of this action. The covenant people of Israel are the recipients of this activity.

Step 3 – Look up the definition: Meaning

Various dictionaries describe this word as sickness, illness, or disease. It is an impairment of health or an abnormal function of the body.

Step 4 – Look up its function: Morphology

The Hebrew morphology: noun, common, masculine, plural, construct. The 'noun' tells us the part of speech. 'Common' informs us that this is a general word for any number of diseases, not one particular illness or medical condition. The grammatical 'masculine' ties 'disease' to the verb and subject of which both are 'masculine.' Here we see word relationships and treat this as a phrase. I can't stress this idea enough, communicate ideas to your audience, not just stand-alone word meanings. 'Plural' informs there are multiple diseases in the meaning. 'Construct' shows a relationship between 'all' and 'your.'

Step 5 – Understand near and far contexts

We must trace this word with a concordance search to

examine every context from Genesis to Malachi. When you do this, you will discover that these types of 'diseases' are not referencing colds, cases of flu, and other common ailments of a fallen world but instead are punishments for Israel when she breaks her covenant as a nation with God. See, in particular, Deuteronomy 29:22–29.

Step 6 – Write out a definition in your own words

The word refers to a sickness connected to breaking God's law and not a reference to a common cold or flu, or any other sickness due to the fall of man. The disease in this context is a punishment for sin, and the only remedy is genuine repentance.

Matthew 8:24, Mark 4:38, Luke 8:23 – Asleep

Step 1 – Start with Action: Verbs

The verb chosen is 'asleep.' In Matthew 8:24 and Luke 8:23, it is the verb of the primary clause, according to *OpenText*. In Mark 4:38, it is the verb of the embedded clause.

Step 2 – Focus on Other Key Words

We will not be focusing on any other keywords for this example. But feel free to look at other words for more practice.

Step 3 – Look up the definition: Meaning

In Luke 8:23, the Greek word is ἀφυπνόω (aphypnoō). This word means to "fall asleep." In Matthew 8:24 and Mark 4:38, the Greek word is καθεύδω (katheudō). This word means to sleep or be asleep.

Step 4 – Look up its function: Morphology

Morphology and context play an important role in understanding the meaning of these two words, but they also help us understand the order of the events described in these three Gospels. In Luke 8:23, the Greek morphology for the word ἀφυπνόω (aphypnoō) is as follows. It is a verb. It is aorist, which means the action took place in the past. It is an active voice, so Jesus is the subject completing the action. Since the word in context means to 'fall asleep' and the narrative states Jesus fell asleep after they sailed, we can presume this event happened before the other two narratives. It is the third person singular, referring to Jesus as the subject.

In Matthew 8:23, the word changes to καθεύδω (katheudō). It, too, is a verb of action. It is imperfect and indicative, which informs us that the action started in the past and continued for a time. It is an active voice, so Jesus is the subject doing the action. Based on our context, this is later chronologically from Luke 8:23. A storm is now taking place on the sea, and the boat "was covered" with waves. It is the third person singular, referring to Jesus as the subject.

We now come to our third context, Mark 4:38. It is the Greek word καθεύδω (katheudō), and it is a verb of action. The morphology reveals it is a present participle. It means the action is taking place in the present, and the action is continuing. It is singular and masculine, which links it to Jesus. It is also nominative, which is the case for the subject, referring back to Jesus as the subject of the action. The context reveals water is now in the boat. So, this follows chronologically after the two narratives. The sleeping will soon end when the disciples wake Jesus up because of being fearful.

Step 5 – Understand near and far contexts

When we examine the three contexts and consider the chronology, with the meaning and morphology, it becomes clear that these Gospels provide details that reveal a series of actions and events. We discover three different snapshots from three distinct moments of Jesus sleeping. Furthermore, if you continue your word studies with the remaining verbs, you will find other details that will paint a more precise timeline and order of events. Thus, these three gospels present a fascinating, successive detailed series of events from the storm on the sea.

Step 6 – Write out a definition in your own words

After you complete your research, it is essential to summarize what you have learned about each word. Your goal is not to focus on these "uncooked raw ingredients of lexical and morphological insights." Instead, through conversational and narrative preaching, place your audience on the ship to experience the events as they occur chronologically.

PRESENTATION

- https://www.DigitalSword.org/wordstudy
- Download the word study worksheet to guide your Bible study.
- Review the training videos to help you integrate word studies as you study with your computer.

SUMMARY

Goal

- To discover, identify, and translate the text's original meaning through word studies and morphological insights.

Strategy
- Properly use tools and resources to determine the meaning of words in the Bible.

Tactics/Assignments
- Choose a passage from the book of the Bible that you will be studying, teaching/preaching
- Identify and determine the meaning of all the verbs for each passage.
- Identify all other significant keywords and their meanings for the passage being studied.
- Review other resources beyond dictionaries for any important word study insights.

Pitfalls & Warnings
- The number one pitfall is introducing too much technical or academic language to the audience. Therefore, be certain you have simplified and integrated the meanings into your message avoiding jargon or difficult-to-understand words.

- The second pitfall is to make your message about word studies and miss the doctrinal and application implications.
- The third pitfall is to lack substance and merely engage with the narrative aspects of the text.
- Do not pronounce the Hebrew and Greek words when you teach or preach unless they sound similar to an English word, are very familiar, or are essential and theologically significant.
- Avoid jumping from one too many texts as you explain the word meanings.
- Look for illustrations in the word studies that can assist in explaining the word to the audience.

EXCEL STILL MORE

- Was the Hebrew or Greek word appropriately pronounced, and did it sound like a familiar English word?
- Was the definition easily understood and

illustrated?

- Was the definition integrated naturally into the flow of the sermon rather than being read from a dictionary, lexicon, or commentary?
- Was the definition accurate and correct for the context?
- Are the most critical words identified in the message?
- Were there too many word studies shared with the audience?
- Was there a balance in the number of cross-references for the word studies?

RECOMMENDED BOOKS

Hebrew Dictionaries and Lexicons

- Baker, Warren and Eugene E. Carpenter. *The Complete Word Study Dictionary*: Old Testament. Chattanooga, TN: AMG Publishers, 2003.
- Blass, Friedrich, Albert Debrunner and Robert

Walter Funk. *A Greek Grammar of the New Testament and Other Early Christian Literature*. Chicago: University of Chicago Press, 1961.

- Brown, Francis, Samuel Rolles Driver and Charles Augustus Briggs. *Enhanced Brown-Driver-Briggs Hebrew and English Lexicon*. Electronic ed. Oak Harbor, WA: Logos Research Systems, 2000.

- Holladay, William Lee, Ludwig Köhler and Ludwig Köhler. *A Concise Hebrew and Aramaic Lexicon of the Old Testament*. Leiden: Brill, 1971.

- Koehler, Ludwig, Walter Baumgartner, M. E. J. Richardson and Johann Jakob Stamm. *The Hebrew and Aramaic Lexicon of the Old Testament*. Electronic ed. Leiden; New York: E.J. Brill, 1999.

- *New International Dictionary of Old Testament Theology & Exegesis*. Edited by VanGemeren,

Willem. Grand Rapids, MI: Zondervan Publishing House, 1997.

- Putnam, Frederic Clarke. *Hebrew Bible Insert: A Student's Guide to the Syntax of Biblical Hebrew.* Quakertown, PA: Stylus Publishing, 2002.

- Swanson, James. *Dictionary of Biblical Languages With Semantic Domains: Aramaic (Old Testament).* Electronic ed. Oak Harbor: Logos Research Systems, Inc., 1997.

- Swanson, James. Dictionary of Biblical Languages with Semantic Domains: Hebrew (Old Testament). Electronic ed. Oak Harbor: Logos Research Systems, Inc., 1997.

- *Theological Wordbook of the Old Testament.* Edited by Harris, R. Laird, Gleason L. Archer, Jr. and Bruce K. Waltke. Electronic ed. Chicago: Moody Press, 1999.

Greek Dictionaries and Lexicons

- Arndt, William, Frederick W. Danker and Walter Bauer. *A Greek-English Lexicon of the New Testament and Other Early Christian Literature*. 3rd ed. Chicago: University of Chicago Press, 2000.
- Balz, Horst Robert and Gerhard Schneider. *Exegetical Dictionary of the New Testament*. Grand Rapids, Mich.: Eerdmans, 1990.
- Chapman, Benjamin and Gary Steven Shogren. *Greek New Testament Insert*. 2nd ed., revised. Quakertown, PA: Stylus Publishing, 1994.
- Brown, Colin. *New International Dictionary of New Testament Theology*. Grand Rapids, MI: Zondervan Publishing House, 1986.
- Friberg, Timothy, Barbara Friberg and Neva F. Miller. Vol. 4, *Analytical Lexicon of the Greek New Testament*. Baker's Greek New Testament library. Grand Rapids, Mich.: Baker Books, 2000.

- Liddell, H.G. *A Lexicon: Abridged from Liddell and Scott's Greek-English Lexicon*. Oak Harbor, WA: Logos Research Systems, Inc., 1996.
- Louw, Johannes P. and Eugene Albert Nida. *Greek-English Lexicon of the New Testament: Based on Semantic Domains*. Electronic ed. of the 2nd edition. New York: United Bible Societies, 1996.
- Lukaszewski, Albert L., Mark Dubis and J. Ted Blakley. *The Lexham Syntactic Greek New Testament: Expansions and Annotations*. Logos Research Systems, Inc., 2010.
- Robertson, A. T. *A Grammar of the Greek New Testament in the Light of Historical Research*, Logos, 1919.
- Swanson, James. Dictionary of Biblical Languages With Semantic Domains: Greek (New Testament). Electronic ed. Oak Harbor: Logos Research Systems, Inc., 1997.

- Thayer, Joseph Henry. *A Greek-English Lexicon of the New Testament:* Being Grimm's Wilke's Clavis Novi Testamenti. New York: Harper & Brothers., 1889.
- *Theological Dictionary of the New Testament.* Edited by Kittel, Gerhard, Geoffrey W. Bromiley and Gerhard Friedrich. Electronic ed. Grand Rapids, MI: Eerdmans, 1964.
- Vine, W. E., Merrill F. Unger and William White, Jr. *Vine's Complete Expository Dictionary of Old and New Testament Words.* Nashville, TN: T. Nelson, 1996.
- Zodhiates, Spiros. *The Complete Word Study Dictionary: New Testament.* Electronic ed. Chattanooga, TN: AMG Publishers, 2000.

CHAPTER FOUR

REMOVING THE VEIL OF BABEL, PART 2

"And how hear we every man in our own tongue, wherein we were born?"

— Crowd at Pentecost, Acts 2:8

PURPOSE

Learn the rules of the original languages of the Bible with Logos Bible Software to ensure a precise understanding of what the original author wrote and meant.

PREPARATION

"The past, present, and future were in an accident; it was a tense moment!" You probably feel just as "tense" about the subject of grammar. If you are like most individuals, English grammar was neither your favorite subject in school nor was it easy. You are probably thinking right at this moment, "There is no way I am going to enter the world of Hebrew and Greek grammar!" But before you skip this chapter, I want to encourage you to read on.

Bible software can bridge the gap between what you need to know and what you do not know. With the right resources and tools, you can easily discover grammatical insights for any passage you are studying. You can be confident that you will rightly divide and understand God's written Word.

There are three critical areas of grammatical studies: lexical (word meaning), morphological (type, form, and function of a word) – these two we have already discussed in the previous chapter, and the third, syntactical (word relationships). The strategy and approach taken in this book are to leverage the grammatical insights of the experts. Not all of us have the time to go back to school and learn Hebrew and Greek grammar from scratch. However, there are excellent resources online and essential books that can assist you in closing the knowledge gap. At the end of this chapter, there will be a list of grammar helps. Growing in grammatical knowledge is vital for understanding the Scriptures.

INSTRUCTION

Getting the Right Resources

Grammar resources fall into six categories: English Grammar for the Original Languages, Beginner Grammar, Intermediate Grammar, Advanced Grammar, Commentaries with grammatical insights, and Specialty Grammars. Each resource is essential for expanding your grasp of Hebrew and Greek grammar. I recommend that you acquire several resources from each category. Let's review several of these resources and discuss how to use them to gain grammatical insights for Bible study.

English Grammars for the Original Languages

These resources are the best place to review grammatical concepts for English. This foundation can help you build a bridge from English to Hebrew and Greek grammatical ideas more easily. For example, the grammatical concept of *number* is essential when determining if the subject is one individual or more than one individual. *Number* is essential to understand when looking at the English pronoun *"you."* You will need to know if "*you*" is singular (one) or plural in number (more than one).

Beginner Grammars

The purpose of these resources is to introduce the Hebrew and Greek language. They typically start with the alphabet, then the various parts of speech such as nouns, verbs, adjectives, etc. These books will provide examples with explanations and sometimes exercises to reinforce the lesson. You will learn vocabulary and important fundamental grammatical concepts critical for understanding how the language works.

Many of these books will spend time explaining morphology and how to "parse" or "recognize" a word so you understand what the word is and how it functions in the sentence. Since you have Bible software, these tools will do this heavy lifting on your behalf. Therefore, avoid memorizing these paradigms in the early stages of learning grammar. Let the computer help you "parse" so that you can focus on interpretation.

Intermediate Grammars

For an in-depth discussion and additional Biblical examples, seek intermediate grammatical resources. These books are more technical in explaining and use technical jargon and academic terms to describe grammatical concepts. They will discuss the more complicated grammatical ideas that beginner grammars ignore. These can be difficult to read, especially if you are new to Hebrew or Greek grammar.

Advanced Grammars

These are the most technical of all the grammatical resources. They are academic, technical, and filled with jargon. They presume the reader has a good grasp of

Hebrew and Greek grammar knowledge. They provide Biblical as well as extra-biblical examples. They will discuss the finer points of the language.

Commentaries with Grammatical Insights

Exegetical commentaries, as well as expositional commentaries, are two rich sources of grammatical insights. These two commentary types will only identify significant grammatical concerns of the text. Their discussions are usually concise and moderately technical but accessible for those committed to learning grammar.

Specialty Grammars

These unique resources will typically focus on one grammatical topic. They usually are academic, technical, and shorter in length. They will serve as specialty supplements in your library of grammatical resources.

APPLICATION

The process outlined below relies heavily on the work of other scholars and Bible software. The goal is to identify significant grammatical insights that clarify the Biblical text. Even though a passage has a lot of grammatical data, we are looking for grammatical data to guide and confirm the author's intended meaning and ensure a correct interpretation. Although there are only two steps in this process, please realize this can be time-consuming for tracking down and seeking clarity on grammatical issues related to the passage.

Psalm 103:1-5

In Step 1, you will look for significant grammatical Constructions. In Step 2, you will look for grammatical insights. Let's examine Psalm 103:1-5 and see what grammatical insights can prove helpful.

Step 1 – Look for Significant Grammatical Constructions

The beginning of Psalm 103:1-2 and the ending of Psalm 103:20-22 utilize an "inclusio." An "inclusio" is like a bracket that places similar material at the beginning and the end. In the case of these passages, "praising the Lord" begins and ends the Psalm and serves as a bracket enclosing the whole Psalm on these actions. These are essentially acting like bookends.

Step 2 – Look for Grammatical Insights

Psalm 103:3 has two grammatically identical phrases. However, their meanings are not similar, but there is a relationship. As mentioned in the previous chapter, the word for "disease" relates to "diseases as punishment for breaking the covenant." The grammatical parallelism reinforces this relationship. See Figures 13-14 to view the relationship between the Hebrew text and morphology for Psalm 103:2.

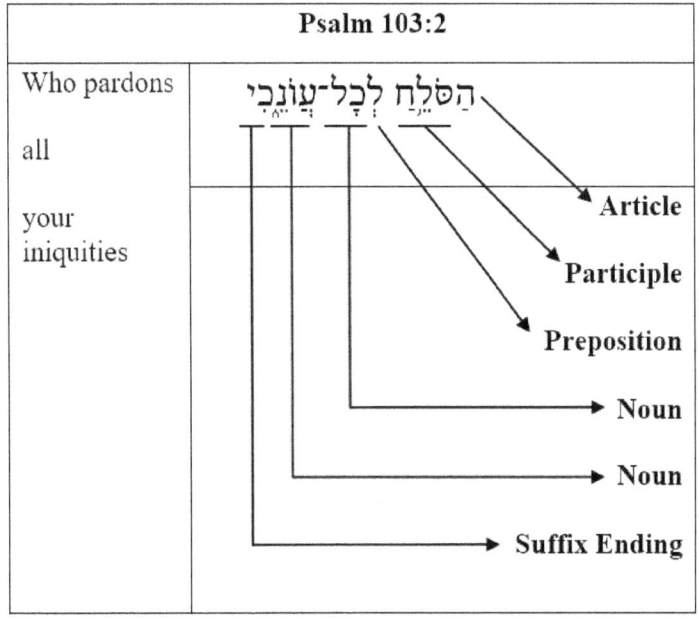

Figure 13. Hebrew text and morphology

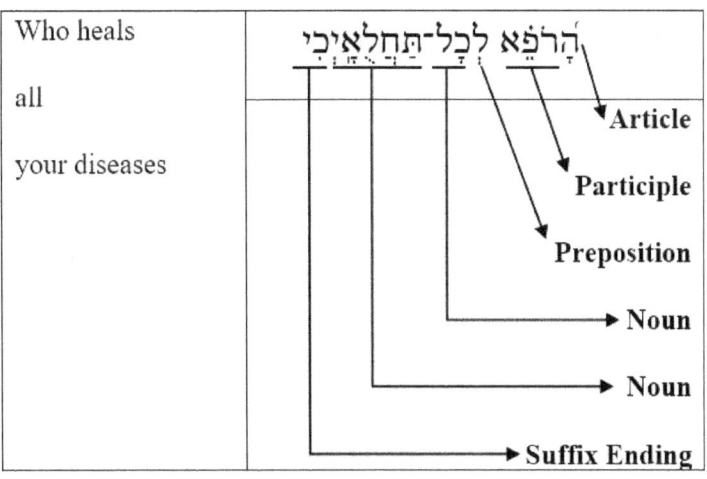

Figure 14. Hebrew text and morphology

By looking at the relationship between the lexical,

morphological, and syntactical, the author's intended meaning becomes more apparent, and the interpretation has a more secure foundation.

Matthew 8:23-27

Let's examine Matthew 8:23-27 and see what grammatical insights can prove helpful.

Step 1 – Look for Significant Grammatical Constructions

Since this is a narrative, the predominant structure will be the flow of the story. Several "clause level connections" link the clause or phrases to show the time progress in the text.

See figures 15 and 16 for examples of connectors (and = καὶ, but = δὲ, so that = ὥστε).

Matthew 8:23 When He got into the boat, His disciples followed Him.	
• When He got into the boat Καὶ ▸ αὐτῷ ἐμβάντι εἰς πλοῖον 1 2 3 2 4 5 **Note:** The numbers represent the Greek word order. **Note:** We did not translate the second phrase to focus on the boat.	**Καὶ** is not translated in the NASB, but it is a conjunction to continue the story.
Matthew 8:24 And behold, there arose a great storm on the sea, so that the boat was being covered with the waves; but Jesus Himself was asleep.	
And Behold, there arose καὶ ἰδοὺ → ἐγένετο 1 2 5	**Καὶ** is translated and continues the events.

Figure 15. Matthew 8:23-24 Grammatical Constructions

DIGITAL SWORD

so that the boat ὥστε τὸ πλοῖον ← 9 10 11	ὥστε is another conjunction and reveals a purpose or result.
but Jesus Himself was asleep δὲ αὐτὸς ἐκάθευδεν • → 17 16 18	δὲ is another type of conjunction showing sequence but with contrast. In this context, the disciples were awake contrasted with Jesus being asleep.

Figure 16. Matthew 8:23-24 Grammatical Constructions

By following these clause-level connections, we can see the phrases and the storyline develop.

Step 2 – Look for Grammatical Insights

In verse 25, the disciples wake Jesus and say, "Save us, Lord; we are perishing!" An excerpt from Moulton's grammar helps us understand the significance and meaning of "perishing":

"A very important example in the NT is the recurrent οἱ

ἀπολλύμενοι "the perishing." Just as much as ἀποκτείνω and its passive ἀποθνῄσκω, ἀπόλλυμαι implies the completion of the process of destruction. When we speak of a "dying" man, we do not absolutely bar the possibility of a recovery, but our word implies death as the goal in sight. Similarly in the cry of the Prodigal, λιμῷ ἀπόλλυμαι, Lk 15:17, **and in that of the disciples in the storm, σῶσον, ἀπολλύμεθα, Mt 8:25, we recognise in the perfective verb the sense of an inevitable doom**, under the visible conditions, even though the subsequent story tells us it was averted." (James Hope Moulton, *A Grammar of New Testament Greek: Prolegomena.*, vol. 1 (Edinburgh: T. & T. Clark, 2006–, 114–115.)

Based on this grammatical insight, we can confirm that the disciples truly believed they would die and the threat of the storm was real.

Now at this point, you are probably saying, "How in the

world do I find this information?" This is where Bible software comes to the rescue. It is capable of quickly finding these examples with little effort. The training videos will show you how to perform these searches.

PRESENTATION

- https://www.DigitalSword.org/grammar
- Download the grammar study worksheet to guide your Bible study.
- Review the training videos to help you integrate grammar studies as you study with your computer.

SUMMARY

Goal

- To discover grammatical insights to understand the Biblical meaning clearly.

Strategy

- Effectively use tools and resources to identify applicable grammatical insights.

Tactics/Assignments
- Choose a passage from the book of the Bible that you will be studying, teaching/preaching.
- Identify and determine any significant grammatical constructions with Bible software.
- Identify and determine any significant grammatical insights from the six types of grammatical resources.

Pitfalls & Warnings
- The number one pitfall is sharing grammatical insights with technical jargon with the audience. Therefore, be sure you have simplified and integrated the grammatical insights into easy-to-understand explanations in a conversational manner.

EXCEL STILL MORE
- Were there any significant grammatical insights overlooked?

- Was technical jargon used to explain grammatical insights that the audience might not understand?
- Did the grammatical insights help the audience make the text more understandable?

RECOMMENDED BOOKS

*Highly recommend resources

English Grammars for Hebrew

- *Long, Gary A. *Grammatical Concepts 101 for Biblical Hebrew*. Second Edition. Grand Rapids, MI: Baker Academic, 2013.
- *Van Pelt, Miles V. *English Grammar to Ace Biblical Hebrew*. Grand Rapids, MI: Zondervan, 2010.
- *Williams, Michael. *The Biblical Hebrew Companion for Bible Software Users: Grammatical Terms Explained for Exegesis*. Grand Rapids, MI: Zondervan, 2015.

English Grammars for Greek
- *Lamerson, Samuel. *English Grammar to Ace New Testament Greek*. Grand Rapids, MI: Zondervan, 2004.
- *Long, Gary A. *Grammatical Concepts 101 for Biblical Greek: Learning Biblical Greek Grammatical Concepts through English Grammar*. Peabody, MA: Hendrickson Publishers, 2006.
- *Strauss, Mark L. T*he Biblical Greek Companion for Bible Software Users: Grammatical Terms Explained for Exegesis*. Grand Rapids, MI: Zondervan, 2016.

Beginner Hebrew Grammars
- Barrett, Michael P. V., and Robert D. Bell. *Bob Jones University Seminary Hebrew Handbook*. Edited by Mary Schleifer. Sixth Edition. Greenville, SC: Bob Jones University Press, 2007.

- Cohn-Sherbok, Dan. *Biblical Hebrew for Beginners*. London: Society for Promoting Christian Knowledge, 1996.
- *Fields, Lee M. *Hebrew for the Rest of Us: Using Hebrew Tools without Mastering Biblical Hebrew*. Grand Rapids, MI: Zondervan, 2008.
- Futato, Mark David. *Beginning Biblical Hebrew*. Winona Lake, IN: Eisenbrauns, 2003.
- Kelley, Page H., Timothy G. Crawford, and Terry L. Burden. *A Handbook to Biblical Hebrew: An Introductory Grammar*. Second Edition. Grand Rapids, MI: William B. Eerdmans Publishing Company, 2018.
- Mansoor, Menahem. *Biblical Hebrew Step by Step*. 2d ed. Vol. 1. Grand Rapids, MI: Baker, 1980.
- Martin, James D. *Davidson's Introductory Hebrew Grammar*. 27th ed. London: T&T Clark, 1993.

- Pratico, Gary D., and Miles V. Van Pelt. *Basics of Biblical Hebrew: Grammar*. Second Edition. Grand Rapids, MI: Zondervan, 2007.
- Putnam, Frederic Clarke. *Hebrew Bible Insert: A Student's Guide to the Syntax of Biblical Hebrew*. Quakertown, PA: Stylus Publishing, 2002.
- Van Pelt, Miles V. *Biblical Hebrew: A Compact Guide*. Grand Rapids, MI: Zondervan, 2012.

Beginner Greek Grammars
- Black, David Alan. *Learn to Read New Testament Greek*. 3rd ed. Nashville, TN: B&H Publishing Group, 2009.
- Chapman, Benjamin, and Gary Steven Shogren. *Greek New Testament Insert*. 2nd ed., revised. Quakertown, PA: Stylus Publishing, 1994.
- Davis, William Hersey. *Beginner's Grammar of the Greek New Testament*. Revised and expanded edition. Eugene, OR: Wipf and Stock

Publishers, 2005.

- Easley, Kendell H. *User-Friendly Greek: A Common Sense Approach to the Greek New Testament*. Nashville, TN: Broadman & Holman, 1994.

- Hadjiantoniou, Dr. George. *Learning the Basics of New Testament Greek*. Chattanooga, TN: AMG Publishers, 1998.

- Long, Fredrick J. *Kairos: A Beginning Greek Grammar*. Mishawaka, IN: Fredrick J. Long, 2005.

- *Mounce, William D. *Greek for the Rest of Us: The Essentials of Biblical Greek*, Second Edition. Grand Rapids, MI: Zondervan, 2013.

- Mounce, William D. *Basics of Biblical Greek: Grammar*. Edited by Verlyn D. Verbrugge. Third Edition. Grand Rapids, MI: Zondervan, 2009.

- Mounce, William D. *Biblical Greek: A Compact*

Guide. Grand Rapids, MI: Zondervan, 2011.

- Parker, David. *Learning New Testament Greek Now and Then*. Sydney College of Divinity Press: Sydney, 2008.

- Schwandt, John D. *An Introduction to Biblical Greek: A Grammar with Exercises*. Bellingham, WA: Lexham Press, 2017.

- Summers, Ray, and Thomas Sawyer. *Essentials of New Testament Greek*. Rev. ed. Nashville, TN: Broadman & Holman, 1995.

- Vine, W. E. *Vine's You Can Learn New Testament Greek!: Course of Self-Help for the Layman*. Nashville, TN: Thomas Nelson, 1996.

- Zacharias, H. Daniel. *Biblical Greek Made Simple: All the Basics in One Semester*. Bellingham, WA: Lexham Press, 2018.

Intermediate Hebrew Grammars

- Van der Merwe, Christo H. J., Jacobus A. Naudé, and Jan H. Kroeze. *A Biblical Hebrew*

- *Reference Grammar*. Second Edition. London; Oxford; New York; New Delhi; Sydney: Bloomsbury; Bloomsbury T&T Clark: An Imprint of Bloomsbury Publishing Plc, 2017.
- *Waltke, Bruce K., and Michael Patrick O'Connor. *An Introduction to Biblical Hebrew Syntax*. Winona Lake, IN: Eisenbrauns, 1990.

Intermediate Greek Grammars

- Black, David Alan. *It's Still Greek to Me: An Easy-to-Understand Guide to Intermediate Greek*. Grand Rapids, MI: Baker Books, 1998.
- Harvey, John D. *Greek Is Good Grief: Laying the Foundation for Exegesis and Exposition*. Eugene, OR: Wipf & Stock, 2007.
- Larkin, William J. *Greek Is Great Gain: A Method for Exegesis and Exposition*. Eugene, OR: Wipf & Stock, 2008.
- Mathewson, David L., and Elodie Ballantine Emig. *Intermediate Greek Grammar: Syntax for*

Students of the New Testament. Grand Rapids, MI: Baker Academic: A Division of Baker Publishing Group, 2019.

- Porter, Stanley E., Jeffrey T. Reed, and Matthew Brook O'Donnell. *Fundamentals of New Testament Greek*. Grand Rapids, MI; Cambridge: William B. Eerdmans Publishing Company, 2010.

- *Wallace, Daniel B. *Greek Grammar Beyond the Basics: An Exegetical Syntax of the New Testament*. Grand Rapids, MI: Zondervan, 1996.

- Young, Richard A. *Intermediate New Testament Greek: A Linguistic and Exegetical Approach*. Nashville, TN: Broadman & Holman, 1994.

Advanced Hebrew Grammars

- Andersen, Francis I., and A. Dean Forbes. *Biblical Hebrew Grammar Visualized*. Edited by M. O'Connor, Cynthia L. Miller-Naudé, and Jacobus A. Naudé. Linguistic Studies in Ancient

West Semitic. Winona Lake, IN: Eisenbrauns, 2012.

- Bodine, Walter R., Monica S. Devens, E.J. Revell, and Edward L. Greenstein. *Linguistics and Biblical Hebrew*. Winona Lake, IN: Eisenbrauns, 1992.
- Gesenius, Friedrich Wilhelm. *Gesenius' Hebrew Grammar*. Edited by E. Kautzsch and Sir Arthur Ernest Cowley. 2d English ed. Oxford: Clarendon Press, 1910.
- *Joüon, Paul, and T. Muraoka. *A Grammar of Biblical Hebrew*. Roma: Pontificio Istituto Biblico, 2006.

Advanced Greek Grammars

- *Blass, Friedrich, Albert Debrunner, and Robert Walter Funk. *A Greek Grammar of the New Testament and Other Early Christian Literature*. Chicago: University of Chicago Press, 1961.
- Guthrie, George H., and J. Scott Duvall. *Biblical

Greek Exegesis: A Graded Approach to Learning Intermediate and Advanced Greek. Grand Rapids, MI: Zondervan, 1998.

- Moulton, James Hope. *A Grammar of New Testament Greek.* 5 Volumes. Edinburgh: T. & T. Clark, 2006.
- Robertson, A. T. *A Grammar of the Greek New Testament in the Light of Historical Research.* Logos Bible Software, 2006.

Commentaries with Grammatical Insights

- See Chapter 8, the recommended books section: exegetical commentaries bibliography.

Specialty Hebrew Grammars

- Miller, Cynthia L. *The Verbless Clause in Biblical Hebrew: Linguistic Approaches.* Vol. 1. Linguistic Studies in Ancient West Semitic. Winona Lake, IN: Eisenbrauns, 1999.
- Freedman, David Noel, A. Dean Forbes, and Francis I. Andersen. *Studies in Hebrew and*

Aramaic Orthography. Vol. 2. Biblical and Judaic Studies. Winona Lake, IN: Eisenbrauns, 1992.

- *Adams, John. *Sermons in Accents: Or, Studies in the Hebrew Text*. London; New York: T&T Clark, 1906.

Specialty Greek Grammars

Campbell, Constantine R. *Basics of Verbal Aspect in Biblical Greek*. Grand Rapids, MI: Zondervan, 2008.

- Porter, Stanley E. *Idioms of the Greek New Testament*. Sheffield: JSOT, 1999.

- Carson, D. A. *Greek Accents: A Student's Manual*. Grand Rapids, MI: Baker Books, 1985.

CHAPTER FIVE

HOP, SKIP, AND JUMP

"In the first year of his reign I Daniel understood by books the number of the years, whereof the word of the Lord came to Jeremiah the prophet, that he would accomplish seventy years in the desolations of Jerusalem."

— Daniel the Prophet, Daniel 9:2

PURPOSE

Learn to identify critical Biblical cross-references to understand the author's intended meaning and related Biblical texts.

PREPARATION

Have you ever tossed a stone across the water? What was your highest number of skips? Five, ten, or more? There are several factors to skip a stone across the water effectively. First, what is the quality of the stone? Is it smooth and appropriately weighted? Is it the right size for your hand and your strength? Do you have the proper throwing technique and angle to the water? What are the conditions of the water? If one of these factors is less than perfect, it will limit how far your stone will hop, skip, and jump before it sinks to the bottom.

Cross-referencing to other Bible passages from your passage can be much like this experience. For some preachers and teachers, they skip from one passage to the next like our stone across the water, and you are not quite sure the kind of stone they are throwing, nor how many skips! Worse, you may take flight with a 'poorly thrown' passage and find yourself sinking in unfamiliar waters!

INSTRUCTION

So, what are the best practices for cross-referencing from one passage to the next? There are four key ideas to consider when cross-referencing. First, we must choose the proper type of cross-reference. Second, we need to determine the purpose of the Biblical cross-reference. Third, we must determine the particular number of Biblical cross-references. Finally, one must choose the optimal placement of the cross-references.

4 Types

Word

There are four general types of cross-references. The first is to cross-reference by a word. For example, you may wish to explain the concept of bond-servant from Romans 1:1. You can accomplish this by cross-referencing another passage that uses this same word, for example, Galatians 1:10.

Phrase

The second type of cross-reference is a phrase. Here you want to find a passage that repeats an idea in the same manner as your passage. For example, the various "I am" passages about Jesus.

Topic/Idea

The third type of cross-reference communicates a topic or idea. These cross-references will likely not use the exact words from your passage, but the concept it conveys must exist in the verse you cite. For example, if you teach and preach from Matthew 28:19-20 and speak about evangelism, you would cross-reference to Acts 17:22-34 and talk about Paul's method of evangelism. Since there can be many topics related to a passage, identify the subject matter to the audience before you cross-reference, ensuring the idea is clearly stated and understood and then linked to the cross-reference cited.

Theological

The fourth type of cross-reference is a cross-reference to a theological idea. This category is vital for teaching doctrine. There are many theological topics and tangents one can take with the Scriptures. However, the thirteen theological themes mentioned in chapter one need to be developed and expressed in every sermon where appropriate. It is vital to consider the theological themes in your cross-references and ensure they align with the theological emphasis in the passage you teach or preach. In chapter seven, we explore the theological background in more depth.

3 Purposes

Repeat

There are essentially three different purposes for a Biblical cross-reference. The first and most frequently used purpose is the cross-reference that repeats or re-states the point of your passage. These types of cross-references reinforce your main idea.

Add

The second type of cross-reference will expand or add to the point of the passage. These cross-references can be helpful if used properly but confusing if not used properly. For example, if you are talking about the miracles of Christ and your cross-references reveal Christ is God, that additional insight helps the reader understand the identity of Christ. It will require some further explanation. But suppose the cross-references include information about judgment and hell. In that case, you are now inserting ideas about retribution and condemnation, two concepts requiring significant explanation to show their relationship to miracles. If you do not "connect the dots" with the audience, they may become confused about what is being emphasized and connected.

Contrast

The third type of Biblical cross-reference is to contrast the point of the passage. One effective way to define an idea is to state what it is not. Therefore, your point may require a cross-reference that expresses the very opposite to communicate the idea of the passage more precisely.

Proper Number of Cross-References

Number

The number of cross-references will vary from sermon to sermon, but I suggest anywhere between one to three cross-references per significant point in your message.

The more selective you are in cross-referencing, the fewer cross-references you will need. Limiting your cross-references leaves more room for explaining the text, which is the priority. Remember that cross-references are tools to support the point and are not the main idea of the message. It may be necessary to break from these recommendations because the context may demand it. For example, a topical study on the tongue or money would require exploring multiple passages to exhaust the Bible teachings on these subjects. Therefore, cross-reference with wisdom and caution!

Placement

Introduce

The first location for a cross-reference is before your explanation. This location will serve to introduce your point. Positioning a cross-reference here can help ready your audience for the main idea.

Supplement

The second location of placement is parallel to your

exposition. This strategy will immediately supplement and support your point. However, be sure your cross-reference flows from the Biblical text so that the relationship between the text preached and the cross-reference cited is truly obvious and apparent to the audience. If you have to explain the cross-reference, consider choosing a different passage.

Summarize

The third location for cross-reference placement is at the end of your main point. A cross-reference placed here will summarize and conclude your point. Your cross-reference should also have a "summarizing" or "concluding" sense, so the audience does not think you are starting a new topic. Choose a passage that ends the discussion clearly and directly.

Conclusion

I recommend using a variety of cross-reference types, placements, numbers, and purposes to guard against being predictable. One last point: even though cross-referencing is one step in our study process, you should be on the lookout for better cross-references for each step. Remember, the purpose of this step is for you to get the bulk of the critical cross-references identified and organized.

APPLICATION

So how do we cross-reference efficiently and effectively? First, you will need two essential resources: a *Bible* with cross-references and *The New Treasury of Scripture Knowledge*. This excellent book will identify cross-references by passage, keyword, and topic. These two resources will help you identify critical cross-references quickly. Let's overview the four steps:

Step 1 – Read the passage and identify the type of cross-reference from your resources.

Step 2 – Determine the purpose of the cross-reference.

Step 3 – Establish and prioritize the number of cross-references.

Step 4 – Choose the optimal location for the cross-reference.

Psalm 103:1

Step 1 – Read the passage and identify the type of cross-reference.

So, let's begin with Psalm 103:1. As you approach this step, you must be mindful of what you have learned. Allow your studies up to this point to guide your search for key-cross references. For example, Psalm 103:1 begins with "Blessed the Lord." This clause is a type of "phrase cross-reference." *The New American Standard, 1995 Edition,* references Psalm 104:1, which also introduces the Psalm. *The New Treasury of Scripture Knowledge* notes Psalm 68:19. This is also a "phrase cross-reference." Let's proceed to step two with these cross-references.

Step 2 – Determine the purpose of the cross-reference.

As mentioned earlier, Psalm 104:1 and Psalm 103:1 utilize the exact phrase "Blessed the Lord, O my soul."

If we were to cite this passage, its use and purpose would be to repeat the idea. However, Psalm 68:19 repeats, "Blessed be the Lord," but adds additional information, "Who daily bears our burdens, The God of our salvation." It will be essential to determine which is best for your message. Psalm 68:19, with the additional information, complements the ideas found in Psalm 103:1-5 and will reinforce these concepts. Let's proceed to step three.

Step 3 – Establish and prioritize the number of cross-references.

After establishing all the possible and potential cross-references with their purpose, one must prioritize which passages are appropriate for the Biblical text. One must be sensitive to avoid sharing too little or too much information with the audience. If you have too few passages and have the time, consider identifying more cross-references. Once you have identified and prioritized your key cross-references, proceed to step four.

Step 4 – Choose the optimal location for cross-reference.

The placement of Psalm 104:1 has two ideal locations; first, as an introduction to show the relationship between these two psalms. Additionally, this verse could supplement the point, revealing how the author begins both Psalms focusing on God. Psalm 69:19 has a beautiful connection to the benefits of Psalm 103.

Matthew 8:23-27

Step 1 – Read the passage and identify the type of cross-reference.

The events in our selected text from Matthew 8:23-27 appear in two other Gospels: Mark and Luke. Most Bibles will provide cross-references to the other Gospel accounts. Therefore, we minimally need to examine each section and note similarities and dissimilarities. For this example, let's focus on the word "windstorm" or "tempest." In Matthew 8:24, the "Great tempest arose on the sea." In Mark 4:37, "A great windstorm arose." In Luke 8:23, "A windstorm came down on the lake." Each cross-reference describes the storm in three different stages. Therefore, we will utilize all three passages when explaining the storm.

Step 2 – Determine the purpose of the cross-reference.

Since each cross-reference has additional information, and all three are needed to understand the progression of events, we must choose "add" as our purpose for the cross-references.

Step 3 – Establish and prioritize the number of cross-references.

All three cross-references are necessary and, therefore, have priority. We could look at the *Bible* and *The New Treasury of Scripture Knowledge* for additional cross-references on storms. Still, for our purpose, it is best to remain in the story and not jump to other Biblical texts to avoid information overload and distract from our central idea. Additionally, we must put these passages in chronological order to help the audience see the progression of the storm's events. The order would be Mark 4:37, with the storm arising. The background of this text reveals the wind coming over the mountains. Luke 8:23 shows the storm was coming down on the lake. Matthew 8:23 demonstrates the storm interacting with the water. With the cross-references established, organized, and prioritized, we need to determine the placement of these texts.

Step 4 – Choose the optimal location for cross-reference.

Since these cross-references explain the events' circumstances as they occur chronologically, they are vital to explain our passage, Matthew 8:23. We will supplement the Biblical texts with these cross-references as they are critical for explaining the Biblical text.

PRESENTATION

- https://www.DigitalSword.org/cross-reference
- Download the cross-reference worksheet to guide your Bible study.
- Review the training videos to help you integrate cross-referencing as you study with your computer.

SUMMARY

Goal

- To discover, identify, and utilize the whole counsel of Scripture through Bible cross-referencing.

Strategy

- Properly use various resources to determine the most significant Bible cross-references for any given passage.

Tactics/Assignments

- Choose a section from a book of the Bible for

teaching or preaching.

- Find at least one cross-reference for each central point in the outline from the following list:

1. Find one cross-reference based on a word
2. Find one cross-reference based on a phrase
3. Find one cross-reference based on a topic
4. Find one cross-reference based on the central theological theme of the main point.

Pitfalls & Warnings

- Cross-referencing has several pitfalls: too many or too few cross-references and weak or inadequate cross-references. Allow for a smooth transition to and from the cross-reference from the exposition. Try to avoid an improper integration of the cross-reference into the sermon. Be thoughtful of where you place the cross-reference and its purpose in the sermon flow to optimize the clarity of the Biblical text.
- Avoid jumping to obscure passages in the Bible

where the audience cannot easily find the verse location. Avoid moving too quickly through cross-references you have cited. Strategically wait for the truth to sink in with the audience. When narrowing your cross-references, choose the most familiar passage to help your audience grasp the point more quickly. CHIASTIC PSALMS: A STUDY IN THE MECHANICS OF SEMITIC POETRY IN PSALMS 1–50. (William Sailer et al., *Religious and Theological Abstracts* (Myerstown, PA: Religious and Theological Abstracts, 2012).)

- Whenever possible, reinforce fundamental doctrines for your audience by reusing key cross-references from previous messages so that your audience may come to memorize them through your teaching and preaching ministry. If your cross-reference needs a significant explanation, then the cross-reference may be too obscure or off-point and may detract from your exposition.

EXCEL STILL MORE

- Were there cross-references for each central point?
- Were these the best possible cross-references?
- Were the cross-references placed strategically in the sermon?
- Which types of cross-references were utilized?
- Did the cross-references serve their purpose?
- Was there a transition to and from the cross-reference?

RECOMMENDED BOOKS

- Anderson, Ken. *Where to Find It in the Bible*. Nashville: T. Nelson Publishers, 1996.
- Burkett, Larry. *The Word on Finances*. Chicago: Moody Publishers, 1994.
- Ehorn, Seth, and Linda Washington. *The A to Z*

Guide to Finding It in the Bible: A Quick-Scripture Reference. Grand Rapids, MI: Baker Books, 2010.

- Elwell, Walter A., and Douglas Buckwalter. *Topical Analysis of the Bible: With the New International Version*. Vol. 5. Baker Reference Library. Grand Rapids, MI: Baker Book House, 1996.

- Kruis, John G. *Quick Scripture Reference for Counseling*. Expanded Edition. Grand Rapids, MI: Baker Books, 2013.

- McCordic, Charles W. *The Thematic Bible: Topical Analysis*. Bellingham, WA: Logos Bible Software, 2007.

- *Smith, Jerome H. The New Treasury of Scripture Knowledge: The Most Complete Listing of Cross References Available Anywhere-Every Verse, Every Theme, Every Important Word.* Nashville TN: Thomas Nelson,

1992.

- Wiersbe, Warren W. *Index of Biblical Images: Similes, Metaphors, and Symbols in Scripture*. Grand Rapids, MI: Baker Books, 2019.

CHAPTER SIX

OPENING UP THE TIME CAPSULE

"These are the generations of the heavens and of the earth when they were created, in the day that the LORD God made the earth and the heavens."

— Moses the Prophet, Genesis 2:4

PURPOSE

Learn significant and relevant historical information related to the Biblical text to clarify the author's meaning.

PREPARATION

History is important. My two favorite quotes regarding the importance of history are as follows:

- "Those who cannot learn from history are doomed to repeat."—George Santayana
- "All history is incomprehensible without Christ." —Ernest Renan

Have you ever participated in opening a time capsule or

found something buried long ago? The experience is exciting and illuminating but also confusing. It is exciting to connect with the past and illuminating to learn about other people living from another time. However, it is confusing when limited historical information results in an incomplete picture of the past. It's like missing a variety of pieces from a puzzle. Do you take the time to know the historical events surrounding the passage you are studying? Without a grasp of the Biblical past, building a bridge of understanding to our present time is nearly impossible.

This lack of information has implications for applying the text as well. For example, which passage would you preach to comfort those facing persecution for their faith? Which verse would you share to encourage believers to contend for the faith against deceivers within the church? If you do not know the Biblical past of Scriptures where believers faced persecution and

OPENING UP THE TIME CAPSULE

deceivers in the church, how can you answer these questions, let alone help someone? This chapter will equip you to study the historical background of any passage.

Historical research is exciting but fraught with dead ends; if you are not careful, you may find yourself chasing rabbits down a rabbit trail. Before you know it, you have spent hours reading nothing relevant to your message. We want to avoid this time-stealing path! So how do you avoid the destination to "Know-Where-Ville," "Time-is-Up-Town," or "Nothing-to-Show-for-it-City"? Let me help you by introducing you to GPS. Before you jump ahead of me on this one, this is not what you think; we will not use some **g**lobal **p**ositioning **s**ystems like Garmin, Tom-Tom, Apple Maps, or Google Maps. Instead, GPS is an acronym for three essential steps for effectively researching Biblical Passage background for any passage.

G: General Background

Let us begin with 'G' for the "General" Background. In most commentaries and study Bibles, you will find an introduction at the front of each book. This introduction includes the historical background of each book of the Bible. This general information is critical to review before studying or preaching a book of the Bible.

P: Present Circumstances

The next is "P" for the "Present" Circumstances. As you accumulate historical information, confirming facts in various resources, one must remember that the goal is not merely to discover interesting historical facts and anecdotes. Instead, it is to find timeless principles applicable to the time in which we live. In digging deeper into the Biblical text, ask the following question: How can one relate and apply the Biblical text to a present situation? You must always be looking for opportunities to build a bridge from the Biblical past to our current time, maybe through a person, place, event, or wisdom principle.

S: Special Categories

The last letter is "S" for "Special" Categories. Although the information will be different for each book of the Bible, the following categories need more in-depth exploration: (1) People, (2) Places, and (3) Events. You must study every person in the Biblical text you are studying, every geographical location cited, and any act or event, large or little, looking for connections between actions and consequences. For example, consider David and Bathsheba's adulterous actions, Uriah's murder, and the results of God's punishment of David. Examine all the relationships, including family, friends, and enemies.

Learn the history of a city. Discover who and where the nearest neighboring communities are and what would eventually happen to that city. For example, Jericho's founding and fall. Regarding events, research further on what led up to the event and what follows the event.

Three Critical Cautions

Exploring the historical background of people, places, and events in the Scriptures is a thrilling adventure and challenging endeavor. However, one must keep three critical cautions in mind before proceeding.

Historical Illumination

First, the historical background *illuminates* the Biblical text. It does not *interpret* the Biblical text. For example, it informs the reader of the historical context but does not determine the passage's meaning. One must remember that the words of Scripture are inspired, God-breathed, and can be studied directly by the reader. In contrast, historical information outside the Bible is second-hand information, and interpretation depends upon various factors. Precision becomes difficult, especially the older and more distant from the historical data in both time and culture.

Historical Confirmation

Second, historical information requires confirmation by multiple experts. One must be aware of a historical bias when confirming dates or details of events. For example, Moses' birth can vary by over one hundred and seventy-five years, depending on the historian. Such a range of starting dates will have significant implications for other Biblical events such as the Exodus and entrance into Canaan.

Historical Clarification

Third, although the historical background is essential for understanding the Biblical context, one must be judicious when sharing historical information with the audience. A key question is whether the historical record clarifies the Biblical text for the audience. Suppose the historical data is exciting or fascinating but does not help the audience understand the author's meaning. In that case, one must consider setting this information aside for more relevant details to expound and explain the Biblical text. In an ideal world, the historical background would be exciting, fascinating, and biblically relevant, providing a deeper understanding of the author's intended meaning.

INSTRUCTION

Three Primary Resources

Where should one seek historical information? There are three primary resources that every student of Scriptures should utilize for this kind of research: background commentaries, Bible dictionaries, and magazines/journals (see the end of the chapter for book recommendations). My favorite go-to resource is a background commentary. These are a must-have resource since they organize the most relevant historical information verse by verse. These books will save you time in locating crucial historical background information quickly, and they filter out unnecessary information not pertinent to the passage you are studying. A second helpful resource is a scholarly Bible dictionary. These books, organized by subject or topic, contain the most relevant details on people, places, events, dates, and other historical information. The third type of resource is historical and archaeological magazines and journals. These resources can range from a general historical overview to very detailed descriptions.

Six Key Historical Areas of Study

What key historical information should one gather and examine when studying a Biblical context? There are six key areas one must explore when doing historical background research: (1) Author of the Bible book/letter, (2) Date of the Bible book/letter, (3) Recipients of the Bible Book/letter, (4) Circumstances surrounding the events and details of the Bible book/letter, (5) Geographical details related to the people, places, and events within the Bible book/letter, and (6) Past/Present/Future details connected to the people, places, and events within the Bible book/letter.

APPLICATION

Researching historical background is relatively straightforward. Gather general historical information and specific historical facts as you move through each step. There are three key steps.

Step 1 – Examine the passage with a Background Commentary

Step 2 – Examine Bible dictionaries for crucial facts

Step 3 – Examine magazines/journals for additional historical insights

Psalm 103:1

Step 1 – Examine the passage with a Background Commentary

- Examine a background commentary and look for comments about a crown. It reflects divine blessing (Psalm 103:4)
- It is uncertain which bird species is in Psalm 103:5; however, a background commentary may provide a few suggestions. We can study birds

in the bible and learn they picture sustaining strength and vigor.

Step 2 – Examine Bible dictionaries for crucial facts

- Use a Bible dictionary and look up 'blessing.' When God is the subject of a blessing, this implies worship is taking place (Psalm 103:1).

- Locate in a Bible dictionary an article on Israel and its history. You will discover that throughout their history, they forget God (Psalm 103:2). The dictionary will provide scriptural references such as Judges 3:7.

- Search a Bible dictionary on healing and a sub-article on God and healing. Throughout Scripture, God is the one who heals, in particular, within the covenant of Israel (Psalm 103:3).

Step 3 – Examine magazines/journals for additional historical insights

- Some magazines and journals will focus on a

specific book in the Bible and provide insights into the historical context. However, sometimes you will come up short. The specific historical context for David writing this Psalm is unknown. The Scriptures reveal this Psalm reflects thanksgiving and praise to God.

- There was a superstition during the medieval age that an eagle renewed its youth every ten years by flying upward into the fiery region beyond the sky and then plunging into the ocean. (See The Faerie Queene by Edmund Spenser, authored in 1590). This tale is exciting, fascinating but not Biblically relevant.

Matthew 8:23-27

Step 1 – Examine the passage with a Background Commentary

- According to *IVP Background Commentary*, only the local people called the lake of Galilee the "Sea of Galilee."

- Background commentaries will reveal how there are many Greek myths describing gods or demigods controlling nature before Christ's time.

Step 2 – Examine Bible dictionaries for crucial facts
- The boat used in this passage was most likely a fishing boat. Use a Bible dictionary to examine articles on boats, particularly fishing boats.
- A Bible dictionary will reveal that the Sea of Galilee is also called the Sea of Gennesaret and is 200-plus meters below sea level. Its low position can result in fast down-winds and intense storms.

Step 3 – Examine magazines/journals for additional historical insights
- Magazines and journal periodicals will reveal that Josephus describes boats that could hold approximately 1000 pounds and include a crew of 10 to 15 people.

- Archeological journals will reveal that the remains of a shipwreck in the sea of Galilee recovered a stone anchor and some pottery.
- Archaeological journals will keep up with the latest historical discoveries, including the discovery of a 2,000-year-old fishing boat in the Sea of Galilee in 1986. It may be very similar to the boat in this passage.

Remember that you may not find much background information as you research the background of your passage. Therefore, don't spend a lot of time researching. Be willing to move on and only utilize historical information that helps clarify the meaning of the text.

PRESENTATION

- https://www.DigitalSword.org/historicalbackground
- Download the historical background worksheet to guide your Bible study.

- Review the training videos to help you integrate historical background research as you study with your computer.

SUMMARY

Goal
- To discover and identify the relevant historical elements for your passage.

Strategy
- Use the passage guide, factbook, and search engine to research the historical background. Examine the introductions from commentaries, Study Bibles, Bible dictionaries, magazines, journals, and OT/NT surveys.

Tactics/Assignments
General (Book of the Bible)
- Choose a passage from the book of the Bible for studying, teaching, and preaching.
- Identify and record the book's author(s) using

the techniques from the training videos.

- Find and document the date range of the Bible book, determine the date of events taking place within the book, and any additional time markers from individual passages.
- Determine the recipients mentioned and where they live geographically.
- Uncover and write down the circumstances surrounding the writing of the particular Bible book you are examining.
- Find a Map and locate where the events took place.
- Examine the website: http://www.hyperhistory.com/online_n2/History_n2/a.html
- Determine what other world events and significant people were living and doing at the time of the book you are studying.

Specific (Biblical Passage you are studying, teaching,

and preaching)

- Research the background for any person, place, and event using the passage guide, Biblical people, Biblical places, and Factbook.
- Identify any additional historically significant material relevant to the passage you are studying.

Pitfalls & Warnings

- The number one pitfall is to skip this step! Therefore, minimally collect this data from the introductory sections of your commentaries and study Bibles.
- The second pitfall is turning these historical insights into a boring lecture. Avoid this by telling a story with the facts placed strategically throughout your message.
- Avoid too much detail and those details not directly tied to the Biblical text.
- Ensure you have thoroughly studied all the

Biblical passages from the OT to the NT on significant people, places, and events. Do not miss an opportunity to show prophecy fulfilled or a significant past or future event related to your passage.

EXCEL STILL MORE

- Was the background of the passage explained and integrated into the sermon properly?
- How was the Biblical past made relevant to our present-day?
- Was the data factually accurate and presented clearly?
- Did the message properly subordinate the historical details to the main point of the Biblical text?
- Did the message miss anything significant historically?
-

RECOMMENDED BOOKS

- Archer, Gleason Leonard. *A Survey of Old Testament Introduction.* 3rd. ed.]. Chicago: Moody Press, 1998.

- Guthrie, Donald. *New Testament Introduction.* 4th rev. ed. The master reference collection. Downers Grove, Ill.: Inter-Varsity Press, 1996.

- Jensen, Irving L. *Jensen's Survey of the New Testament: Search and Discover.* Chicago: Moody Press, 1981.

- Jensen, Irving L. *Jensen's Survey of the Old Testament: Search and Discover.* Chicago: Moody Press, 1978.

- Keener, Craig S. *The IVP Bible Background Commentary: New Testament.* Second Edition. Downers Grove, IL: IVP Academic: An Imprint of InterVarsity Press, 2014.

- MacArthur, John. *The MacArthur Bible Handbook.* Nashville, TN: Thomas Nelson

Publishers, 2003.

- Matthews, Victor Harold, Mark W. Chavalas, and John H. Walton. *The IVP Bible Background Commentary: Old Testament*. Electronic ed. Downers Grove, IL: InterVarsity Press, 2000.

- Rusten, Sharon with E. Michael. *The Complete Book of When & Where in the Bible and throughout History*. Wheaton, IL: Tyndale House Publishers, Inc., 2005.

- Walton, John H. *Zondervan Illustrated Bible Backgrounds Commentary* (Old Testament): 6 Volumes. Grand Rapids, MI: Zondervan, 2009.

- Wilkinson, Bruce, and Kenneth Boa. *Talk Thru the Bible*. Nashville: T. Nelson, 1983.

- Willmington, H. L. *Willmington's Bible Handbook*. Wheaton, Ill.: Tyndale House Publishers, 1997.

CHAPTER SEVEN

SEEING THE FOREST AND THE TREES

*"Study to shew thyself approved unto God,
a workman that needeth not to be ashamed,
rightly dividing the word of truth."*

— Paul the Apostle, 2 Timothy 2:15

PURPOSE

Learn to identify significant theological themes and insights related to the passage you are studying to see a connection between near and far Biblical contexts.

PREPARATION

The academic term 'theology' may bring to mind the hallowed halls and classrooms of professors and students arguing over nuances of interpretation and jousting with jargon to win an argument. However, I promise you that you will have no such experience in this chapter. Instead, I want to open up a new vista of insight when you study the Scriptures.

If you have studied the Bible for any time, you have experienced examining one passage and beginning to recall related Bible verses. The more you study, the more connections you will see. Exploring theology can help you see and organize those connections more quickly. Additionally, it can help you reason through difficult passages and protect you from contradicting another portion of the Bible.

Think of theology as a series of significant Bible themes or topics. Specific Bible passages shed more or less light on a particular theological theme. A theology book will focus on various theological themes/doctrines and provide additional Scriptures related to your passage, helping you connect the verse you are studying to a larger Scriptural theme/doctrine. In other words, theology can help you see the proverbial "forest through the trees." What are the top theological themes? You might recall them from chapter 1.

Table 15. Theological Themes

13 THEOLOGICAL THEMES	
01 Bibliology / The Bible	08 Anthropology / Man
02 Theology / God the Father	09 Hamartiology / Sin
03 Christology / God the Son	10 Soteriology / Salvation
04 Pneumatology / God the Spirit	11 Israelology / Israel
05 Cosmology / Spiritual & Material World	12 Ecclesiology / The Church
06 Angelology / Angels	13 Eschatology / Future
07 Demonology / Satan and Demons	

But these themes of theology are also thirteen interpretive questions. For example, as you read the Scriptures, ask the following question, "Does this verse discuss one of these theological themes, say Jesus Christ (Christology)?" If it does, note what you learn and write down that specific passage. When you study with these thirteen questions in mind, you will be thrilled at how much Scripture has to say about each of these topics. Before you know it, you will think theologically!

The Bible was progressively unveiled to the world. It took over 1400 years to finish; over 40 authors from different times and cultures were involved and written in three languages: Hebrew, Aramaic, and Greek. And yet, there is unity amid the diversity. Therefore, theological doctrines develop and grow in detail from book to book. For example, if you study Jesus Christ (Christology), you will learn something in nearly every book of the Bible: who He is, when He will come, how He lived and died, and how He will come again to rule and reign! Wow!

Studying theology requires a systematic, consistent Bible study approach. When preparing your message, you must see the big picture, connecting not just to the chapter and book you are studying but to all the books of the Bible. You want to discover the theological theme in your passage and then begin to trace this theme through other books of the bible to study more in-depth. If all you had in hand were the Bible, this would be a daunting task, but if you have several theology books, your task is much easier than you realize!

One more additional thought. Most passages in the Bible introduce more than one theological theme. However, there is usually one primary doctrine that will stand out more than the others. You can identify the central theological doctrine with the following questions:

- What is the most referenced/discussed theological theme of the paragraph?
- Do other doctrines support or point to the primary theological doctrine?

- What is the new or additional information about a particular theological doctrine?
- Is the doctrine being used to argue a point?
- Is the doctrine being used to reinforce or conclude?

As you can see, having a good grasp of theology is vital to interpreting Scripture. Now, I must give a warning. Theology is to flow out of Scripture and not into Scripture when studying and interpreting. Too many teachers and preachers allow their "theology" to "inform" or "bias" their interpretation and make the passage say something the original author never intended. This theological partiality can blind you to the correct interpretation. So be careful! Let's now prepare for an exciting adventure into the realm of theology!

INSTRUCTION

The process of identifying theological themes in a single passage is very straightforward. You read the passage and look to see which of the thirteen theological themes is referenced. Before diving into our OT and NT passages, let me give you an example.

Step 1 – Read the passage

Let's choose a very familiar passage, John 3:16 "For God so loved the world, that He gave His only begotten Son, that whoever believes in Him shall not perish, but have eternal life." (NASB95)

Step 2 – List the theological themes

I typically move from word to word, then phrase to phrase. The first key phrase is "God loved." Since this references God the Father, I will add to my list below "Theology." The next words to follow are "the world." This expression references man, not material creation, so choose "Anthropology." The following words "He gave His." These pronouns reference God the Father. The phrase "Only begotten Son" is a reference to Jesus Christ, "Christology." The next key idea is "whoever." This word could reference "man" or "the church."

However, since the context is not about the church but people in general, let's choose "man" or "Anthropology." The next action is "believes" and is connected to faith and, in this context, salvation, "Soteriology." The following phrase is "in Him" and represents the object of faith: Jesus Chris, "Christology." The final two expressions, "shall not perish" and "have eternal life," describes two places, Hell and Heaven. We could choose "cosmology" since these are places, but we could select "eschatology" since it represents a future event. In situations like this, I put both down. Here is our list for John 3:16. By the way, if you are typing these out, I recommend you list them by the academic term first. In most word processors, you can sort by paragraph, automatically arranging them and making it easy to spot the most repeated. This strategy is essential for large verse ranges.

My List

- Theology / God the Father / "God loved"
- Anthropology / Man / "The World"
- Theology / God the Father / "He Gave"
- Christology / God the Son / "Only Begotten Son"
- Anthropology / Man / "Whoever"
- Soteriology / Salvation / "Believes"
- Christology / Christ / "In Him"
- Cosmology / Hell and Heaven / "shall not perish, but have eternal life"
- Eschatology / Judgment / "shall not perish, but have eternal life"

Step 3 – Choose the primary and secondary theological themes

This step will examine our sorted list and look for the most repeated theological themes.

My List (Sorted)

- (2x) Anthropology / Man / "The World"
- Anthropology / Man / "Whoever"

- (2x) Christology / Christ / "In Him"
- Christology / God the Son / "Only Begotten Son"
- (1x) Cosmology / Hell and Heaven / "shall not perish, but have eternal life"
- (1x) Eschatology / Judgment / "shall not perish, but have eternal life"
- (1x) Soteriology / Salvation / "Believes"
- (2x) Theology / God the Father / "God loved"
- Theology / God the Father / "He Gave"

In our list, Man, Christ, and Theology repeat twice. Additionally, we must also consider the main action in this passage, which is "loved" and "gave." "Perish" and "have" are subordinate ideas based on the *OpenText* clause analysis. Therefore, the main theological themes are God and Christ. If we read the passage in light of these two choices, God is the primary, and Christ is the secondary emphasis.

Final List

Primary Theological Theme: God the Father

Secondary Theological Theme: God the Son, Jesus

At this point, we would search our systematic theology resources and review "Theology" and "Christology" connected to "love" and "gave" to find other related passages to these theological themes. Furthermore, we could search for salvation and faith too. In the end, we are looking to deepen our understanding of God's love and Christ's sacrifice regarding man's salvation and faith.

APPLICATION

Psalm 103:1-5

Step 1 – Read the Passage

Step 2 – List the Theological Themes

Psalm 103:1
- Theology / God the Father / "Bless the Lord"

- Anthropology / Man / "O my soul"
- Anthropology / Man / "all that is within me"
- Theology / God the Father / "bless his holy name"

Psalm 103:2

- Theology / God the Father / "Bless the Lord"
- Anthropology / Man / "O my soul"
- Theology / God the Father / "forget none of his benefits"

Psalm 103:3

- Theology / God the Father / "Who"
- Soteriology / Salvation / "pardons"
- Hamartiology / Sin / "all your iniquities"
- Theology / God the Father / "Who"
- Cosmology / Spiritual & Material Universe / "heals"
- Hamartiology / Sin / "all your diseases"

Psalm 103:4

- Theology / God the Father / "Who"

- Soteriology / Salvation / "redeems"
- Hamartiology / Sin / "your life from the pit"
- Theology / God the Father / "Who"
- Soteriology / Salvation / "crowns"
- Anthropology / Man / "you"
- Soteriology / Salvation / "lovingkindness and compassion"

Psalm 103:5
- Theology / God the Father / "Who"
- Cosmology / Spiritual & Material Universe / "satisfies your years with good things"
- Anthropology / Man / "so that your youth is renewed"
- Cosmology / Spiritual & Material Universe / "the eagle"

Step 3 – Choose the primary and secondary theological themes
- Primary: Theology / God the Father
- Secondary: Anthropology / Man

- Tertiary: Soteriology / Salvation
- Quaternary: Hamartiology / Sin

Matthew 8:23-27

Step 1 – Read the Passage

Step 2 – List the Theological Themes

Matthew 8:23

- Christology / God the Son / "He got into"
- Cosmology / Spiritual & Material Universe / "the boat"
- Anthropology / Man / "His Disciples followed Him"

Matthew 8:24

- Cosmology / Spiritual & Material Universe / "And behold, there arose a great storm on the sea, so that the boat was being covered with the waves"
- Christology / God the Son / "Jesus Himself was asleep"

Matthew 8:25

- Anthropology / Man / "And they came to Him and woke Him, saying, "save us Lord; we are perishing"
- Christology / God the Son / "Him" & "Lord"

Matthew 8:26

- Christology / God the Son / "Why are you afraid"
- Anthropology / Man / "you men of little faith"
- Christology / God the Son / "Then He got up and rebuked"
- Cosmology / Spiritual & Material Universe / "The winds and the sea, and it became perfectly calm"

Matthew 8:27

- Anthropology / Man / "The men were amazed"
- Christology / God the Son / "what kind of a man is this, that even the winds and the sea obey Him"

- Cosmology / Spiritual & Material Universe / "winds and the sea"

Step 3 – Choose the primary and secondary theological themes
- Primary: Christology / God the Son
- Secondary: Cosmology / Spiritual & Material Universe
- Tertiary: Anthropology / Man

PRESENTATION
- https://www.DigitalSword.org/theology
- Download the theology worksheet to guide your Bible study.
- Review the training videos to help you integrate theology as you study with your computer.

SUMMARY

Goal
- To discover and identify the relevant theological elements for your message.

Strategy

- Use the theological custom guide and collection tools with the search engine to research your theological background.

Tactics/Assignments

- Choose a passage from the book of the Bible that you will be teaching and preaching.
- Identify all the theological categories mentioned above for each passage.
- Identify the two most important theological themes for your passage.
- Create a collection of all your theology books and add it to your passage guide.
- Using the custom guide with your theology collection, search your passage and find two additional key verses for each theological doctrine you identified in the passage you are studying.

Pitfalls & Warnings

- The number one pitfall is to introduce to the audience too many theological doctrines; therefore, be certain you have chosen one doctrine, and it is the primary doctrine.
- The second pitfall is to turn this message into an academic lecture on theology rather than showing the practical relevance of this doctrine to your hearers.
- Avoid providing too many cross-references for your key or supporting doctrine to your audience.
- Ensure you study the doctrine and fully comprehend the topic and its implications to avoid contradicting the Scriptures.
- Time permitting, read several opposing views to your doctrine to be aware of any controversies or opposing arguments.

EXCEL STILL MORE

- Was the primary theological theme identified?

- Was the theological background of the passage explained and integrated into the sermon properly?
- How was the theological theme made relevant to our present day?
- Was the theological theme factually accurate and presented clearly?
- Did the message properly subordinate the other theological themes of the Biblical text?
- Did the message miss anything significant theologically?

RECOMMENDED BOOKS

- Allison, Gregg R. *Sojourners and Strangers: The Doctrine of the Church*. Edited by John S. Feinberg. Foundations of Evangelical Theology Series. Wheaton, IL: Crossway, 2012.
- Berkhof, L. *Systematic Theology*. Grand Rapids, MI: Wm. B. Eerdmans Publishing Co., 1938.
- Boice, James Montgomery. *Foundations of the*

- *Christian Faith: A Comprehensive & Readable Theology*. Downers Grove, IL: InterVarsity Press, 1986.
- Calvin, John, and Henry Beveridge. *Institutes of the Christian Religion*. Edinburgh: The Calvin Translation Society, 1845.
- Carson, D. A., ed. *NIV Biblical Theology Study Bible*. Grand Rapids, MI: Zondervan, 2018.
- Cole, Graham A. *He Who Gives Life: The Doctrine of the Holy Spirit*. Edited by John S. Feinberg. Foundations of Evangelical Theology. Wheaton, IL: Crossway Books, 2007.
- Cottrell, Jack. *The Faith Once for All: Bible Doctrine for Today*. Joplin, MO: College Press Pub., 2002.
- Culver, Robert Duncan. *Systematic Theology: Biblical and Historical*. Ross-shire, UK: Mentor, 2005.
- Demarest, Bruce A. *The Cross and Salvation:*

The Doctrine of Salvation. Foundations of Evangelical Theology, Wheaton, IL: Crossway Books, 1997.

- Elwell, Walter A. *Evangelical Dictionary of Biblical Theology*. Electronic ed. Baker Reference Library. Grand Rapids: Baker Book House, 1996.

- Elwell, Walter A and Douglas Buckwalter. *Topical Analysis of the Bible: With the New International Version*. Vol. 5. Baker Reference Library. Grand Rapids, MI: Baker Book House, 1996.

- Enns, Paul. *The Moody Handbook of Theology*. Edited by Jim Vincent and Allan Sholes. Revised and Expanded. Chicago, IL: Moody Publishers, 2014.

- Erickson, Millard J. *Christian Theology*. 2nd ed. Grand Rapids, MI: Baker Book House, 1998.

- Feinberg, John S. *Light in a Dark Place: The*

- *Doctrine of Scripture*. Edited by John S. Feinberg. Foundations of Evangelical Theology. Wheaton, IL: Crossway, 2018.
- _____. *No One Like Him: The Doctrine of God*. The Foundations of Evangelical Theology. Wheaton, IL: Crossway Books, 2001.
- Frame, John M. *Systematic Theology: An Introduction to Christian Belief*. Phillipsburg, NJ: P&R Publishing, 2013.
- _____. *The Doctrine of God. A Theology of Lordship*. Phillipsburg, NJ: P&R Publishing, 2002.
- _____. *The Doctrine of the Christian Life. A Theology of Lordship*. Phillipsburg, NJ: P&R Publishing, 2008.
- _____. *The Doctrine of the Knowledge of God. A Theology of Lordship*. Phillipsburg, NJ: P&R Publishing, 1987.
- _____. *The Doctrine of the Word of God*. A

Theology of Lordship. Phillipsburg, NJ: P&R Publishing, 2010.

- Geisler, Norman L. *Systematic Theology, Four Volumes*. Minneapolis, MN: Bethany House Publishers, 2002.
- Grudem, Wayne A. *Systematic Theology: An Introduction to Biblical Doctrine*. Leicester, England; Grand Rapids, MI: InterVarsity Press; Zondervan Pub. House, 2004.
- Henry, Carl F. H. *God, Revelation, and Authority*. Wheaton, IL: Crossway Books, 1999.
- Packer, J. I. *Concise Theology: A Guide to Historic Christian Beliefs*. Wheaton, IL: Tyndale House, 1993.
- MacArthur, John, and Richard Mayhue, eds. *Biblical Doctrine: A Systematic Summary of Bible Truth*. Wheaton, IL: Crossway, 2017.
- Reymond, Robert L. *A New Systematic Theology of the Christian Faith*. Nashville: T.

Nelson, 1998.

- Ryrie, Charles Caldwell. *Basic Theology: A Popular Systematic Guide to Understanding Biblical Truth*. Chicago, IL: Moody Press, 1999.

- Shedd, William Greenough Thayer. *Dogmatic Theology*. Edited by Alan W. Gomes. 3rd ed. Phillipsburg, NJ: P & R Pub., 2003.

- Swindoll, Charles R., and Roy B. Zuck. *Understanding Christian Theology*. Nashville, TN: Thomas Nelson Publishers, 2003.

- Van Til, Cornelius. *An Introduction to Systematic Theology*. The Presbyterian and Reformed Publishing Company: Phillipsburg, NJ, 1979.

- Wellum, Stephen J. *God the Son Incarnate: The Doctrine of Christ*. Edited by John S. Feinberg. Foundations of Evangelical Theology Series. Wheaton, IL: Crossway, 2016.

CHAPTER EIGHT

DOUBLE TAKE

"These were more noble than those in Thessalonica, in that they received the word with all readiness of mind, and searched the Scriptures daily, whether those things were so."

— Luke the Physician, Acts 17:11

PURPOSE

Learn to utilize commentaries to check and correct your research.

PREPARATION

In the popular secular Christmas song "Santa Claus is Comin' to Town," we learn that "Santa is making a list and checking it twice, gonna find out who's naughty or nice." When it comes to your commentary work, we, too, are faced with the same task. In hand, we have our preliminary outline, word studies, historical background, theological background, cross-references, and additional observations, insights, and conclusions. In front of us are the various commentaries with the same information. Now we must "check our work twice" and see if our interpretations are "naughty or nice," that is to say, have we faithfully observed and interpreted the Biblical text up to this point in our studies?

Self-Bias

At this stage, we have three obstacles to a proper interpretation. First is the barricade of our "self-bias." With our research before us and the time investment behind us, we may feel confident we have arrived at what the text communicates. However, we must continue asking the question, "Am I correct in my interpretation; am I accurately handling the Word of God?" We must be good Bereans and fight for accurate illumination and competent exegesis. One way to ensure a Biblical interpretation is to look at the Biblical evidence supporting your interpretation. We believe what we have been taught but rarely know the "why" behind the "what." We must especially guard against this kind of bias. We don't start with the premise "I know what the text means." Instead, we set aside our current understanding of the text, and restudy afresh as if this is the first time we have examined this passage. I sometimes even approach a familiar text and try to prove my interpretation is wrong for argument's sake. I'll even read opposing views. This strategy keeps me honest and open with the text so that I consider all the Biblical evidence.

Expert-Bias

The second hurdle to overcome is "expert-bias." Here, we may hold a particular publisher(s) or author(s) in high esteem. We will weigh their words more heavily and significantly in the interpretative process. We may even change our earlier conclusions from our studies because of their influence. It is important to discern when an author contributes to the text's clarity, providing genuine Biblical evidence and accurately reflecting the Biblical meaning. Therefore, we must hold all referenced sources to a high standard and guard against the "infallibility factor" in which "they are always right, and never wrong!"

Audience-Bias

The third barrier is "audience bias." This bias is a genuinely dangerous threat because of its persuasive powers. The seeking of men's approval over God's approval has caused many individuals to succumb to this siren call. We know the pressure people can apply to a church, teacher, or leader to hold to a particular view. Beware of those inside and outside the church who reject sound doctrine. Many of these people may be looking for their ears to be tickled, accumulating teachers who will vindicate their unrighteous desires and justify false beliefs or incorrect theology. Like the crack in the dam that springs a leak, one small compromise after another will, in time, destroy the integrity of the message, the messenger, and hearers, until a furious flood washes away any traces of Biblical truth, Holy Worship, diligent discipling, and evangelistic efforts. As the dam crumbles, so will the lifetime work of a comprised, man-centered ministry. As our Lord so pointedly revealed, a house built on the Rock, the Word of God, will endure, but any other foundation is sinking sand, washed away in the end. I should also add that not all compromises will be this obvious. Doctrinal shifts may subtly enter the scene, such as a word change or simply avoiding the discussion altogether.

So how do we maintain balance and integrity in the cross-checking process, seeking God's approval along the way, staying steadfastly faithful to the Biblical text, and, all the while, counting down the minutes before the next message? Prayer! Patience! Perseverance! To guide you through this process, I recommend you review figure 17, the anatomy of a commentary, to help you check your work for each category, ensuring you have reviewed every aspect of your research thoroughly.

Figure 17. Anatomy of a Commentary

INSTRUCTION

As you have realized, commentaries arrive at the end of the study process rather than at the beginning. This approach is by design. I can't stress this enough, guard yourself against studying with commentaries first. You will never develop good study habits nor learn critical thinking skills, and you will be dependent more on men than the Holy Spirit for illumination. Of course, there are always exceptions and times when you may need to start with commentaries.

To use commentaries effectively, it goes without saying that you must have the best commentary resources. In this chapter's recommended book section, I have suggested several resources that recommend and review commentaries for each book of the Bible to guide you in your purchases. Based on their input, I highly recommend building a library comprising three commentary types: concise, exposition, and exegetical commentaries.

7 Key Areas of Review

There are seven key areas to consider in the review process. Let's begin with the foundational first step, your outline.

A. Outline

In this step, you must confirm that you have selected the appropriate verse range. For example, if you are preaching Matthew 28:19-20 and you neglect Matthew 28:16-18, you have failed to choose the full context and, therefore, are ignoring significant and relevant Biblical material, including the "authority" of Christ. At this step, you want to determine that your significant points are the same vital points the commentaries address. It's a good idea to examine the commentaries' outline and see if your outline is similar. Although there may be some minor differences, confirm that you are not introducing outlier ideas in your outline or that you are majoring on points that are considered minor or insignificant.

B. Word Studies

This step is straightforward. You need to confirm that your definitions are accurate and reflect the original meaning. Note any significant insights you may have missed, any illustrations, analogies, or cross-references that further clarify your word studies. The goal here is not to be more technical but to present the Biblical text more clearly, conversational, and relatable to the audience.

C. Grammar

At this stage, you are looking for additional grammatical insights you may have missed during your studies. Try not to get bogged down in the technical discussions but rather look for grammatical insights and explanations to increase your understanding of the text, which affirm the authorial intent and meaning of the Biblical text.

D. Historical

Occasionally, commentaries provide historical background for a person, place, event, or general context. These historical insights are invaluable and, if engaging, are highly prized for preaching and teaching. These are relatively easy to spot and should not require much time to locate as you work through the commentary verse by verse.

E. Theological

This step is challenging because each commentator has their own theological bias. Therefore, you will need to be discerning regarding their theological insights. Furthermore, examine the cross-references and argumentation to justify the author's position. Do not be too quick to rush in and embrace any theological points unless the exegesis can support their stance.

F. Cross-References

This step is the easiest of all the steps. All that is required is to look up the passage and confirm if it explains the Scriptures more clearly than your other cross-references. The goal here is to choose the "best of the best."

G. Argument/Logic

This step is probably the most difficult of all the steps. You will need to analyze all the arguments and evidence. You are like a judge hearing both sides of the case with all the evidence presented. Sometimes there is minimal argument or proof. On the other hand, there can be too many arguments, and the evidence is overwhelming. Therefore, I recommend constructing a pro/con list. First, write down what you or the commentary is trying to prove in one sentence. This sentence could be in the form of a question or statement.

- **Question:** In Genesis 1:5, what does " day" mean?
- **Statement:** In Genesis 1:5, a day represents 24 hours.

Then in the "pro" column, you list <u>only Biblical evidence</u> that supports the idea. In the "con" column, you list <u>only the Biblical evidence</u> contrary to the idea. Once you have gathered all the evidence, then you weigh the evidence. The one with the most proof or most robust case wins the argument. I can not stress the importance of reasoning through a difficult passage with this methodology. You will be better prepared to reason with others and handle new evidence and arguments more effectively. Furthermore, it will help you from being ignorant and prideful due to the complexity of some Biblical issues.

As you work with commentaries, you may find along the way other helpful material, such as pictures, tables, illustrations, quotes, and applications. Always be on the lookout for material that will help the audience see the Biblical text more clearly.

APPLICATION

Due to the nature of this section, I will leave the application section blank for both passages so that you can fill it in with the commentaries you have in your possession.

Psalm 103:1-5

Outline – What changes will you make to your outline?

Word Studies – What additional insights and improvements will you formulate for your word studies?

Grammar – Any additional grammatical insights?

Historical – Did you find any new historical insights?

Theological – Are there theological insights you may have missed or need refining?

Cross-References – Were you able to identify better cross-references?

Argument/Logic – Can you improve your arguments and reasonings?

Matthew 8:23-27

Outline – What changes will you make to your outline?

Word Studies – What additional insights and improvements will you formulate for your word studies?

Grammar – Any additional grammatical insights?

Historical – Did you find any new historical insights?

Theological – Are there theological insights you may have missed or need refining?

Cross-References – Were you able to identify better cross-references?

Argument/Logic – Can you improve your arguments and reasonings?

PRESENTATION

- https://www.DigitalSword.org/commentaries
- Download the commentary worksheet to guide your Bible study cross-checking.
- Review the training videos to help you review your research as you study with your computer.

SUMMARY

Goal
- To discover, identify, and utilize the whole counsel of Scripture through a Bible cross-checking process to ensure a clear articulation

of the author's intended meaning of the Biblical text.

Strategy

- Properly use various resources to confirm, correct, and/or add to your exposition of the Biblical text and complete the exposition of the Biblical text.
- Tactics/Assignments
- Choose a passage from the book of the Bible that you will be teaching and preaching
- Interrogate the commentaries as follows:
- Confirm and refine your outline to have the proper divisions within the chosen context
- Confirm and refine your word studies to reflect the text
- Confirm and refine any significant grammatical insights affecting the interpretation
- Confirm and refine your historical insights
- Confirm and refine your theological theme

- Identify and possibly replace any necessary cross-references
- Confirm and refine the interpretive logical flow and conclusions you have made regarding the text
- Identify any meaningful illustrations, quotes, or applications

Pitfalls & Warnings

- The number one pitfall is to jump to the commentaries first.
- The second pitfall is to consult too few or inadequate commentaries, thus not significantly verifying your exposition up to this point
- The third pitfall is relying on one particular author, while evidence from other commentaries is weighted unequally.
- The fourth pitfall is introducing bias, subjectivity, or ignoring evidence during the checking process.

EXCEL STILL MORE

- Did the exposition clearly explain the text?
- Did any of the exposition significantly underplay or overemphasize elements of the Biblical text?
- Was there a consistent, logical, rational flow and explanation of the Biblical text's meaning?
- Was the most relevant information to the Biblical text presented? In other words, could something have been left out, and was something irrelevant added to the exposition? Vice versa, was something left out that would have altered the meaning of the exposition?
- Was the exposition obvious and predictable, lacking depth so that anyone with a cursory reading of the text could have reached the same conclusions?
- Could someone read a study Bible and receive more in-depth insights and teaching?

- Were the elements of the exposition properly integrated, avoiding a technical lecture and presenting the Biblical text as profound, applicable, meaningful, and relevant?

RECOMMENDED BOOKS

Commentary Reviews

- Longman, Tremper, III. *Old Testament Commentary Survey*. Fifth Edition. Grand Rapids, MI: Baker Academic, 2013.
- Carson, D. A. *New Testament Commentary Survey*. Seventh Edition. Grand Rapids, MI: Baker Academic, 2013.
- Rosscup, Jim. *Commentaries for Biblical Expositors: An Annotated Bibliography of Selected Works*. The Woodlands, TX: Kress Christian Publications, 2004.

Concise Commentaries

- Biblical Studies Press. *The NET Bible First*

Edition Notes. Biblical Studies Press, 2006.

- MacArthur, John F., Jr. *The MacArthur Study Bible: New American Standard Bible.* Nashville, TN: Thomas Nelson Publishers, 2006.

- MacDonald, William. *Believer's Bible Commentary: Old and New Testaments.* Edited by Arthur Farstad. Nashville: Thomas Nelson, 1995.

- Packer, J. I., Wayne Grudem, and Ajith Fernando, eds. *ESV Global Study Bible.* Wheaton, IL: Crossway, 2012.

- Walvoord, John F., and Roy B. Zuck, Dallas Theological Seminary. *The Bible Knowledge Commentary: An Exposition of the Scriptures.* Wheaton, IL: Victor Books, 1985.

- Constable, Tom. *Tom Constable's Expository Notes on the Bible.* Galaxie Software, 2003.

Expositional Commentaries

- *James Montgomery Boice Expositional*

Commentary. Grand Rapids, MI: Baker Books.

- *MacArthur New Testament Commentary*. Chicago: Moody Press.

- *Preaching the Word*. Wheaton, IL: Crossway Books.

- *The New American Commentary*. Nashville, TN: B&H Publishing Group.

Exegetical Commentaries

- *A Commentary on the Greek Text. New International Greek Testament Commentary*. Grand Rapids, MI; Carlisle, Cumbria: W.B. Eerdmans; Paternoster Press.

- *International Critical Commentary*. New York: C. Scribner's Sons.

- **Evangelical Exegetical Commentary*. Bellingham, WA: Lexham Press.

- *Hermeneia—a Critical and Historical Commentary on the Bible*. Minneapolis, MN: Fortress Press.

- *The New International Commentary on the Old Testament*. Grand Rapids, MI: Wm. B. Eerdmans Publishing Company.
- *The Pillar New Testament Commentary*. Grand Rapids, MI; Nottingham, England: William B. Eerdmans Publishing Company.
- *Word Biblical Commentary*. Dallas: Word.

DIGITAL SWORD

CHAPTER NINE

VIRTUAL REALITY: ILLUSTRATING IN MULTISENSORY MODE

"A word fitly spoken is like apples of gold in pictures of silver."

— Solomon the King, Proverbs 25:11

PURPOSE

Learn to find, select, and communicate with illustrations that clarify the Biblical text.

PREPARATION

Illustrations are contemporary bridges to the ancient Biblical text. They can help us connect Biblical truths of the past to our present lives. The most crucial attribute of an illustration is to illuminate the text. Just as a flashlight illuminates an area for our eyes to see more clearly, so does a suitable illustration illuminate our minds to understand the Bible better. Illustrations are multifaceted, like a specially prepared diamond; they can take many forms and shapes, each refracting the light with precision and clarity.

Illustrating a Biblical truth is a wonderful way to engage the audience by invoking emotions, encouraging more in-depth thought, and inspiring them to the profound significance and implications of God's Word for their personal life. Illustrations do not necessarily need to be elaborate. My advice is to keep it as simple as possible. Beware of any illustrative imagery that eclipses the Biblical truth, taking the audience's eyes off God and His Word. One must guard against the temptation to control or manipulate the audience with emotional imagery. Exploiting the audience in this manner undercuts the authority of God's word. It creates distrust between the preacher and the audience. It trivializes the truth. Therefore, choose your illustrations carefully! Examine your motives and manner when selecting an illustration. See figure 18 near the end of this chapter for a breakdown of the elements of an

VIRTUAL REALITY: ILLUSTRATING IN MULTISENSORY MODE
illustration.

Two Different Contexts

Before you hunt for illustrations, you need to understand two different contexts. First is the context of the Biblical text, and the second is the context of your teaching setting. For the first context, is the audience or teachings in the Biblical text applicable to the believer or unbeliever? Regarding the second context, are you addressing believers or unbelievers in your audience? Many preachers have taken truths intended for the unbeliever and applied them to the believer, as well as the reverse, applying truths intended for believers and applying them to unbelievers. This kind of inverse application is wholly inappropriate. For example, why would a born-again believer need to repent again for salvation? Or how can an unbeliever obey God if they have never truly repented and believed? So be deliberate and precise and apply Biblical truth to the appropriate audience.

Placement of the illustration

The next step is deciding the placement of the illustration. The introduction and conclusion are natural places for an opening or closing illustration. They can be a superb device for preparing the audience, creating curiosity about what is ahead, or summarizing the essence of a critical point. Just as the worship songs ready our hearts and minds for the preaching event, so does the illustrations that opens the message. The concluding illustration is a wonderful way to make the Biblical text more memorable for the audience, allowing the important ideas to "echo within" throughout the week. One of the most effective illustrations for introducing and concluding a sermon is the "book-end" illustration. This kind of illustration comes in two parts. If you have heard of the radio host Paul Harvey, he was a master of this technique. The radio show would begin with the first half of a story, then he delivered the news of the day, and then the show would conclude with the final half of the story. This strategy would keep the listener engaged from beginning to end.

Purpose of the Illustration

The third step is to determine the purpose of the illustration. The illustration is to make the Biblical text more prominent and clearer in the listener's mind, so you will need to decide if the illustration will repeat the point of the Biblical text, add to the point, or contrast the point. And remember, the Biblical text should be more memorable than the illustration.

The Five Senses

The fourth step involves the five senses: seeing, smelling, hearing, touching, and tasting. I am not suggesting that you arrive in the pulpit perfumed and ready to present a five-course meal. Instead, consider the words you choose, the audience's imagination, and collective experiences as you convey the illustration. The more senses you can invoke and the more alive and memorable the description, the more striking the audience's experience will be. If you effectively use language this way, your word pictures will clarify the Biblical text for the audience and keep them engaged. Don't be afraid to modify, color, and enhance the sermon with visual and audible stimuli. If you are wondering how to illustrate the other senses, such as smell, taste, and touch, it is best to invoke imagery of a shared experience. For example, if you were to invoke the imagery of a pepperoni pizza by describing the smooth melted cheese, the hot spice of pepperoni, the thick tomatoey sauce, and the first bite that burns the roof of your mouth! Are you hungry for a pizza right now? Are you wincing simultaneously and feeling as if the roof of your mouth was just burned? This is how we involve the other senses.

Types of Illustration

The fifth step is to identify the type of illustration you will share. From fact to fiction, stories to quotes, and historical past to the present, make sure the illustration chosen flows with your exposition. Be careful of a forced transition that will be abrupt to the audience.

Emotional Content

The sixth and final step is to choose the emotional content of the illustration. This step is so critical. Your illustration should parallel the emotional tone of the Biblical text. If Paul is serious, then so should the illustration. This principle is not a rigid rule that you cannot break but be careful, for example, when using humor with a serious subject. Be sensitive and deliberate in your choices and ensure your illustrations coordinate and align with the Biblical text's emotions. Illustrations are not just for preachers and teachers. They are fantastic tools for sharing the Gospel and helping you reinforce Biblical truths for personal application. It is worth the extra effort to discover illustrative ways to communicate the transcendent truths of the Bible.

INSTRUCTION

Finding an appropriate illustration can be time-consuming. The methodology proposed below may not always save you time, but it will help you "zero in on" the truth you wish to illustrate.

Step 1 - Write Down Your Point

It is difficult enough to find an illustration, but it is even more difficult if you don't have a specific point in mind. Therefore, you must have identified the text's primary idea that you wish to illustrate. I recommend that you write this out in a single sentence.

Step 2 - Determine the Audience in the Biblical Context

Re-examine the Biblical text and determine who is the one in focus and what their context is. Is it Israel, the Church, the nations, or an individual? Are they a believer or an unbeliever? What is happening in the narrative? What are the circumstances surrounding the Biblical text? You must understand the original audience, and their original context. Write down the setting and circumstances surrounding the Biblical text you are studying in one to four sentences.

Step 3 – Determine the Audience in the Preaching Context

In many preaching and teaching settings, there is a mixture of believers and unbelievers. Amongst believers, there can be a wide range of spiritual maturity. With this in mind, you must ensure your illustration targets the right individuals, being sensitive to various spiritual conditions in the audience. Be aware of your audience's extensive spectrum of cultural, social, educational, and economic differences. The most effective illustrations connect at the level of the broadest shared experience. Therefore, know your audience so that you are relating to as many individuals as possible. Write down in one to four sentences your audience's current setting and circumstances.

Step 4 - The Mind and The Heart (emotions &

affections)

Let me clarify this section. We are not seeking an emotional experience, nor are we looking for a way to manipulate others at the emotional level. Instead, we seek God through His Word with the help of His Spirit to speak directly into our lives. We are seeking for our whole being to experience transformation into Christ-likeness.

However, we must begin with ourselves. If we who preach and teach God's Word remain unchanged by the Biblical text in our studies, should we expect others to experience real and substantive change? When communicating with others, we do not speak to just one part of the person but the whole person on every level, intellectually and emotionally. Remember that collecting facts and confirming data produces a "head" message with "no heart."

VIRTUAL REALITY: ILLUSTRATING IN MULTISENSORY MODE

Studying and approaching God in His Word with the Holy Spirit's help is as much an intellectual exercise as a relational experience. We must avoid quenching or grieving the Holy Spirit as He illuminates us about our life before God and others. We must guard against refusing the transforming work of the Word and Spirit in our lives. We must be devotional and worshipful in our studies. We must avoid a study process that is purely an academic pursuit to produce a speech. Therefore, as you worship through studying and seek to be transformed through God's word, write down the truths that confronted you or impacted you significantly. Write down the emotions you felt as you worked through the text. Write down the steps you did take, are taking, or will take to resolve the gap between the truths you learned and the life you are living.

Step 5 - Determine Location, Purpose, Influence
Before you begin to construct your illustration, you must determine the location of the word picture. The

two most prominent and popular positions are the introduction and the conclusion. For illustrating within the message's body, you can place your illustration before, after, or during a significant point in your message. Avoid illustrating minor points in your message. Once you determine the position, seek out its purpose. Are you looking to introduce, reinforce, or conclude the main point of the message? With location and purpose in hand, one must consider the influence of the illustration. In other words, what do you want the illustration to accomplish with the audience? What are you targeting in your word picture? What truth must they understand? What affections are you addressing? What do you hope will be the godly response to the illustration? Please don't lose sight that the illustration must first and foremost clarify the text meaningfully so that they are engaged and impacted more by the truth than the image you present.

VIRTUAL REALITY: ILLUSTRATING IN MULTISENSORY MODE

Step 6 - Begin Small

When constructing an illustration, start small. Start with a basic analogy. For example, if I wanted to illustrate that something is hot, I would choose fire and state the following, "It is hot like fire." This first step is critical in building illustrations because it forces you to be rooted in a specific reality familiar to most people. Without this first step, one tends to be too general and broad in their thinking, and it becomes difficult later to narrow down the idea.

Step 7 - Build on a Shared Experience & Involve the Senses

As you proceed to illustrate, you must build from a shared experience. Seek to tap into those experiences that are common to all. In a richly diversified church, this can be challenging. Nevertheless, reflect on experiences familiar to most of the audience so that your illustration is relatable to the largest number of people in your audience. It is vital that whatever occasion you choose to build on, it points back to the Biblical text. Jesus did this in His parables, teachings, and conversations. Write down a setting with circumstances for an illustration and then look for connections from your text, your audience, and your word picture to ensure they are related to one another so that the Biblical text is more understandable and clear. Review what you have just written and add additional words to capture the five senses: seeing, hearing, smelling, touching, and tasting. Look for specific vocabulary that can make the experience feel like they are reliving the experience.

Step 8 - Test the Illustration

Once you have formulated your illustration, test it. You can say it aloud to yourself or share it with someone else. Once others hear the example, watch their response closely and ask what you are illustrating. If they identify the point from the Biblical text, you have found a winner!

Step 9 - *Dead End?*

If, after multiple attempts, you cannot find an illustration, don't illustrate. Do not feel obligated to tell a story or provide a word picture. Not every point needs illustrative support! Remember, the Word of God has power, not your words or your illustration. However, if you forgo an illustration, double-check your message and confirm your points are clear.

APPLICATION

Psalm 103:1-5

Step 1 – Write Down Your Point
- Remember the Lord's benefits

Step 2 – Determine the Audience in the Biblical Context
- A believing Israelite worshipping the Lord in light of God's covenant with Israel

Step 3 – Determine the Audience in the Preaching Context
- A believing Christian worshipping the Lord in

light of the New Covenant in Christ

Step 4 – The Mind and The Heart
- Two key emotions regarding my salvation: Gratitude and Thankfulness

Step 5 – Determine Location, Purpose, Influence
- Location: Introduction
- Purpose: Help others reflect on their salvation
- Influence: Cultivate gratitude and thanksgiving

Step 6 – Begin Small
- Being delivered from sin is like being delivered out of a house on fire
- Being delivered from sin is like when Israel was delivered from the Egyptian taskmasters

Step 7 – Build on a Shared Experience & Involve the Senses
- Being delivered from an addiction
- Surviving a car accident
- Surviving a serious health problem
- Working for a terrible boss

Step 8 – Test the illustration
- Find several individuals to share your illustration
- Listen to the feedback and make adjustments

Step 9 – Dead End?
- Was the illustration clear & convincing (Y / N)
- Was the illustration overpowering?
- Would it be better not to illustrate?

Matthew 8:23-27

Step 1 – Write Down Your Point
- Not trusting the Lord when fearful

Step 2 – Determine the Audience in the Biblical Context
- A believing Israelite disciple, weak in faith, following Jesus physically

Step 3 – Determine the Audience in the Preaching Context
- A believing Christian disciple, weak in the faith, following Jesus spiritually

Step 4 – The Mind and The Heart
- Two key emotions: fear and faith

Step 5 – Determine Location, Purpose, Influence
- Location: Conclusion
- Purpose: Help others face their fear and pray rather than panic
- Influence: Cultivate prayer in times of great distress

Step 6 – Begin Small
- I lost my job and began to pray and seek the Lord for help

Step 7 – Build on a Shared Experience & Involve the Senses
- Losing a job
- Death of a spouse
- A significant disease or cancer

Step 8 – Test the illustration
- Find several individuals to share your illustration

- Listen to the feedback and make adjustments

Step 9 – Dead End?
- Was the illustration clear & convincing (Y / N)
- Was the illustration overpowering?
- Would it be better not to illustrate?

PRESENTATION
- https://www.DigitalSword.org/illustrating
- Download the illustrating worksheet to guide your Bible study.
- Review the training videos to help you find and integrate illustrations as you study with your computer.

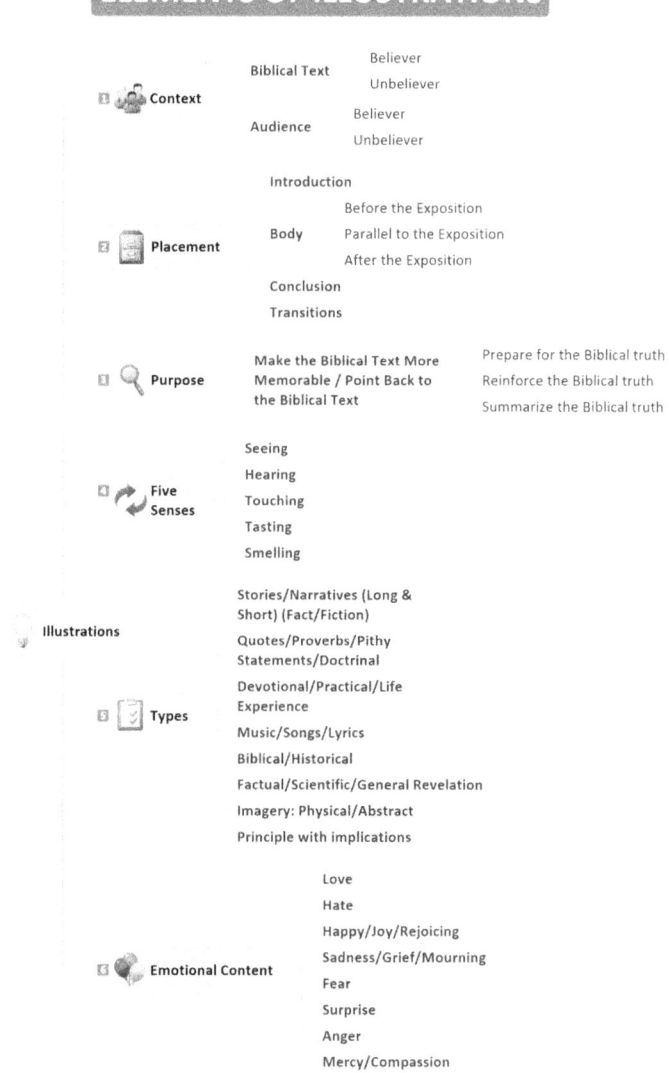

Figure 18. Elements of Illustrations

VIRTUAL REALITY: ILLUSTRATING IN MULTISENSORY MODE

SUMMARY

Goal

- Discover, identify, and utilize illustrations to illuminate, arouse, and enliven the heart, soul, and mind and connect with the Biblical text.

Strategy

- Properly use the five senses to make the Biblical text more clear and relatable to the individual preparing and receiving God's Word.

Tactics/Assignments

- Choose a significant point from your outline and its associated truth from the Biblical text's exposition that will be emphasized and reinforced.
- Determine the audience in the Biblical text, believer or unbeliever.
- Determine who is your target audience, believer or unbeliever, or both.
- Determine the strategic placement of the

illustrations in the sermon.

- Choose the purpose of the illustration: introduce, conclude, reinforce, or contrast.
- Identify any applicable emotion in the Biblical context and convey that tone to the audience.
- Choose the type of illustration. See figure 18 for the general categories.
- Modify or enhance the illustration with word choices to involve the five senses

Pitfalls & Warnings

- The number one pitfall is to have too many or too few illustrations.
- The second pitfall is to make the illustration so powerful that it is more memorable than the Biblical text preached.
- The third pitfall is to rely on the illustrations to communicate the Biblical truth. Make sure your exposition is clear without the illustration.
- The fourth pitfall is to mix, contradict, or

confuse the Biblical text's emotional tones with the illustration.

- The fifth pitfall is to "wing it" and rely on the "moment" for a "Holy Spirit" inspired illustration. Although providence may prompt you to draw from previous experiences, preparation and planning are preferred.

EXCEL STILL MORE

- Did the illustration clearly explain the text?
- Did the illustration significantly underplay or overemphasize elements of the Biblical text?
- Was there a good transition between the illustrations and the Biblical text?
- Was the illustration believable and relatable?
- Did the illustration engage the audience in a meaningful and thoughtful manner?
- Was the illustration manipulative?
- Additional ideas about illustrations, including warnings: See Berkley, James D., ed. *Preaching*

to Convince.

RECOMMENDED BOOKS

- Galaxie Software. *10,000 Sermon Illustrations*. Biblical Studies Press, 2002.

- Jones, G. Curtis. *1000 Illustrations for Preaching and Teaching*. Nashville, TN: Broadman & Holman Publishers, 1986.

- Larson, Craig Brian. *750 Engaging Illustrations for Preachers, Teachers & Writers*. Grand Rapids, MI: Baker Books, 2002.

- Larson, Craig Brian, and Phyllis Ten Elshof. *1001 Illustrations That Connect*. Grand Rapids, MI: Zondervan Publishing House, 2008.

- Michael P. Green. *1500 Illustrations for Biblical Preaching*. Grand Rapids, MI: Baker Books, 2000.

- Moody, D. L. *Anecdotes and Illustrations of D. L. Moody Related by Him in His Revival Work*. Edited by J. B. McClure. Chicago: Rhodes &

McClure, 1878.

- _____. *Anecdotes, Incidents, and Illustrations.* Chicago; New York; Toronto: Fleming H. Revell, 1898.

- _____. *Moody's Stories: Being a Second Volume of Anecdotes, Incidents and Illustrations.* New York: Fleming H. Revell, 1899.

- PreachingToday.com. *Perfect Illustrations: For Every Topic and Occasion.* Wheaton, IL: Tyndale House Publishers, Inc., 2002.

- Ritzema, Elliot, ed. *300 Quotations and Prayers for Christmas.* Pastorum Series. Lexham Press, 2013.

- _____. *300 Quotations for Preachers.* Bellingham, WA: Lexham Press, 2012.

- _____. *300 Quotations for Preachers from the Early Church.* Pastorum Series. Bellingham, WA: Lexham Press, 2013.

- _____. *300 Quotations for Preachers from the Reformation.* Pastorum Series. Bellingham, WA: Lexham Press, 2013.
- Ritzema, Elliot, and Rebecca Brant, eds. *300 Quotations for Preachers from the Medieval Church.* Pastorum Series. Bellingham, WA: Lexham Press, 2013.
- Ritzema, Elliot, and Elizabeth Vince, eds. *300 Quotations for Preachers from the Modern Church.* Pastorum Series. Bellingham, WA: Lexham Press, 2013.
- _____. *300 Quotations for Preachers from the Puritans.* Pastorum Series. Bellingham, WA: Lexham Press, 2013.
- Spurgeon, C. H. *Feathers for Arrows.* London: Passmore & Alabaster, 1870.
- _____. *300 Sermon Illustrations from Charles Spurgeon.* Edited by Elliot Ritzema and Lynnea Smoyer. Bellingham, WA: Lexham

Press, 2017.

- Tan, Paul Lee. *Encyclopedia of 7700 Illustrations: Signs of the Times*. Garland, TX: Bible Communications, Inc., 1996.
- Torrey, R. A. *Anecdotes and Illustrations*. New York: Fleming H. Revell Co., 1907.
- Wilson, Jim L. *300 Illustrations for Preachers*. Edited by Elliot Ritzema. Bellingham, WA: Lexham Press, 2015.

DIGITAL SWORD

CHAPTER TEN

LIVING PROOF: INCARNATING THE LIVING WORD

"I beseech you therefore, brethren, by the mercies of God, that ye present your bodies a living sacrifice, holy, acceptable unto God, which is your reasonable service. And be not conformed to this world: but be ye transformed by the renewing of your mind, that ye may prove what is that good, and acceptable, and perfect, will of God."

— Paul the Apostle, Romans 12:1-2

PURPOSE

Learn to rightly apply the Word of God for inner and outer life transformation into Christlikeness.

PREPARATION

"God is so sovereign that He will use my obedience and disobedience to accomplish His purpose and will...I'd rather have Him use my obedience!"

Application is where the "rubber meets the road," when the "walk meets the talk." It is indisputable proof of a transformed life. It is the salt and light for others to taste and see that the Lord is good! Applying God's word at the individual level must be absent of all hypocrisy. A life of integrity can change the course of history. It must incarnate Christ and His Word to the world. Godly living confirms the message's authenticity and messenger, so the lost might repent and believe. And yet, if one listens to a typical sermon on Sunday in the local church or streams a message online, most sermon applications are man-centered rather than God-centered. It is more about "You" than "Do." All too often, the message is about "living for self" rather than "dying to self." If we profess Christ to the world, we must present Christ and His word in us to the world. Since Christ sacrificed Himself for others, we, His Church, must love and sacrifice for each other and the lost for the sake of the Gospel. If we are to experience substantive transformation in our lives for others to see, we must ensure the application is rooted in an exegetically accurate exposition of the Biblical text. It is important to note that abiding in Christ and His word matters for the here and now and has enormous implications for our future judgment and reward. In 2 Corinthians 5:10-11 and Romans 14:10-13, Paul discusses Christ's judgment seat. It is the place where Christ will examine our Christian life of works and reward us justly apart from sin. In 1 Corinthians 3:5-17, Paul reveals that Christ will judge the fruits of our labor. May our service be appraised as gold, silver, and precious stones, not wood, hay, or stubble! After Christ examines all of our works, the unrewardable and worthless become ashes, but what remains will be our reward. Furthermore, our position and service in the future Millennial Kingdom (Revelation 20:1-10) will be determined in part by our faithfulness and service to Christ in this life.

So how does one know which works will be rewardable

or worthless? The following four questions can guide you in ensuring the application of God's word in your life is rewardable. First, are you seeking the glory of God or the glory of self? Second, are you being guided by the wisdom of God or the wisdom of self? Third, are you empowered by the power of the Holy Spirit or the power of your flesh? Fourth, are you motivated by a love for God and others or yourself? I challenge you to boldly examine yourself in the light of these four questions to glorify God as He rewards you for being a good and faithful servant. Considering these implications, how do we observe Scriptures to gain applicational insights from God's wisdom for our life?

Three Types of Applications

There are three types of applications to observe in the Scriptures. First, we must look at the **patterns** of people. There is a full spectrum of behaviors in the Bible, from obedience to disobedience and everything between these possibilities. Patterns will emerge if we study these individuals in their Biblical context. These examples can guide us on what to embrace and what to avoid. We can learn from a hundred lifetimes of experience by diligently studying these lives within these Biblical accounts.

Besides patterns of people, we can see **principles** in the text. A Biblical principle is a rule of wisdom. They are for guidance as well as avoidance. They can range from what to think, what to say, what to do, and what not to do. One can derive Biblical principles from an extensive study of various passages to form rules, axioms, and proverbs to evaluate any circumstance and determine the best course of action that centers on glorifying God.

The third type of application is a direct **imperative** from God. A Biblical imperative is a clear and explicit command of Scripture, the "do and don't" of the

Biblical text. Imperatives are clear, concise, and non-negotiable. We prove our love for God and individuals in the world by walking obediently to the Scriptures' following Christ's example, and following godly patterns, principles, and imperatives in the Bible. Our faith must be genuine and not motivated by the approval of others. Our obedience is rooted in a deep appreciation for our redemption. Our serving flows from our love and gratitude for the immense gift of God's Son and His sacrifice for our salvation, sanctification, and glorification!

So what hinders us from applying God's truth when it is for our ultimate good and God's glory? My first answer to this question would begin with a wrong understanding of Scripture. Scripture is light, but if we misunderstand Scripture, that light can dim or, worse, be shut off, leading us out of the light and into darkness. Misapplying God's word distorts our thinking, living, and witnessing. Furthermore, a wrong view of Scripture can interfere with our motivation and steer us imperceptibly into sin. Beware of the lust of the eyes and flesh and the pride of life that may reign over our affections and actions. Beware of becoming shortsighted and even blind to Christ's forgiveness of your sin due to a lack of diligence and vigilance in supplying to your faith virtue, knowledge, self-control, perseverance, brotherly kindness, and love (2 Peter 1:5-11). Guard against the downward fleshly and carnal spiral into the misery and bondage of sin. Instead, be filled with the Spirit, yielding to God, turning from sin, and obeying the Word in fear and trembling as God works to accomplish His will in your life for His good pleasure. May God transform your thinking, speaking, and behaving so that others will see Christ in you. May your faith grow through the application of God's Word!

INSTRUCTION

The following strategies will help you discover applications from the Biblical text. See figure 19 near the end of this chapter before the summary section for the "elements of an application."

Foundations for Building Scriptural Applications

A proper foundation must be in place to please the Lord when constructing an application to grow in godliness. The following five principles are essential as you apply the Biblical text.

1. The Word of God is your authority

Your application must be rooted and grounded in the Scriptures. Study the Biblical text and determine the Biblical author's intended meaning and the original audience's application. Once the ancient application is rightly understood, build a bridge to our present time. Be careful not to apply commands strictly for Israel to the Church. Additionally, do not apply texts for unbelievers to believers. Look for principles that transcend time and culture. For example, do not lie or love one another are transcendent principles for any time and culture.

Galatians 5:19-26 compares the works of the flesh with the fruit of the Spirit. This passage is an important reminder that our service unto the Lord must flow from the filling of the Spirit. This filling is only possible when we yield to God's Word by God's power and obey. The Scriptures say it this way "…work out your salvation with fear and trembling for it is God who works in you both to will and to do for His good pleasure." (Philippians 2:12-18). There are only two paths to walk: the Spirit's path or the fleshly path.

2. Christlikeness is the final form

There is a multitude of passages that encourage and instruct us to grow into Christlikeness. Each of us begins as spiritual newborn babes needing the milk of the Word to mature. The Apostle Paul urges us not to be children tossed in every direction but rather to develop into the mature stature of the fullness of Jesus Christ in faith and knowledge of Him (Ephesians 4:13).

3. The goal is to glorify God

It is one thing to know that God is to receive glory by your obedience, but it is another thing to live to the glory of God. Paul summarizes the full scope of our obedience to glorify God in 1 Corinthians 10:31, "Therefore, whether you eat or drink, or whatever you do, do all to the glory of God." In Romans 12:1-2, Paul adds additional insight into the cost of a life devoted to glorifying God, "I beseech you therefore, brethren, by the mercies of God, that you present your bodies a living sacrifice, holy, acceptable to God, which is your reasonable service. And do not be conformed to this world, but be transformed by the renewing of your mind, that you may prove what is that good and acceptable and perfect will of God." This passage affirms the moment-to-moment challenge set before us to deny ourselves, carry our cross, and follow Jesus. Every area of your life is a channel and opportunity for you to glorify the Lord. Seeking to glorify the Lord in all things can bring great joy and meaning to every area of your life, pleasing the Lord and even receiving a future reward.

4. Sacrificial love is the means

The theme of sacrifice is not limited to denying oneself but extends to loving others. Biblical love is not primarily an emotional response but an act of one's will and affection. The story of the good Samaritan demonstrates this principle. His compassion sparks an act of his will, whereby he sacrifices his time, talents, and treasures to rescue a complete stranger. In Acts 4, we see the early church sharing and selling their personal property and even giving the proceeds to the church leadership for distribution to those who need it most in the church body. Epaphroditus, a believer and friend to the Apostle Paul, nearly died (Philippians

3:29-30), serving Paul for the work of Christ. Those who genuinely love others will not merely love with word or tongue alone but will love sacrificially in deed and truth (1 John 3:18).

5. Remember your future reward at the judgment seat.

Future accountability has a way of immediately impacting the decisions we make daily. We can plan for the future more strategically when we have a perspective that extends beyond our immediate gratification. Much of our grief today is the direct result of ungodly disobedience of poor and unwise decisions of the past. We must look to our future judgment soberly, solemnly, and scrupulously and reexamine every aspect of our life. As mentioned early, everything you have thought, said, did, and failed to do will be examined at the judgment seat of Christ and rewarded accordingly. May your reward be plentiful as you hear the Lord Jesus say, "Well done, good and faithful slave.

You were faithful with a few things; I will put you in charge of many things; enter into the joy of your master." (Matthew 25:23).

Steps for Building Scriptural Applications

We will illustrate these steps with Philippians 2:5-11.

Step 1 – Determine the application principle from the text

A. Identify and note the primary theme in the passage

- Theme: Humility

B. Identify and document the primary subject in the passage

- Subject: Jesus

C. Identify and record the actions of the subject in the passage

- Actions: Humbled Himself to death on a cross.

D. Identify and note the various outcomes, effects, implications, and purposes of the subject's actions in the passage. Be sure to examine the full context. Also, look at near and far Biblical contexts for all the "causes and effects" related to the subject's activities.

- Outcome: Reconciliation of sinful man to holy God

Step 2 – Choose the direction of the application principle

A. Vertically – The application will direct individuals to apply the principle in their relationship with God.

- Vertically: God

B. Horizontally – The application will direct individuals to apply the principle in their relationship with believers and unbelievers.

- Horizontally: Other people (spouse, boss, family, neighbor, believer, unbeliever, etc.)

Step 3 – Write out the application principle

A. Generalize the subject, action, outcome

- Vertical: I/You, Humble, reconciliation with God
- Horizontal: I/You, Humble, Reconciliation with others

B. Write out the principle.

- "Without humility, there can be no reconciliation."

Principles are powerful tools for thinking and living and should be concise and memorable.

Step 4 – Confirm from Scripture the application principle

The context of Philippians 2 is about Christ reconciling sinful man to holy God. You and I could never accomplish this task. However, we can seek to resolve our conflicts with one another. Romans 12:18 confirms this principle, "If possible, so far as it depends on you, be at peace with all men."

Step 5 – Consider Illustrating the application principle

After providing a principle to your audience, it can be helpful to illustrate the principle. Let me demonstrate from Philippians 2:5-11:

Imagine a flight of stairs. At the top is Christ, who is God infinite. You and I are at the bottom of the stairs, mere finite mortals. Christ, in humility, comes down the stairs and serves us. He humbles himself by dying on the cross and reconciling sinful man to holy God. We were once His enemy, but now He has made peace through the blood of the cross. Had Christ not humbled Himself, our salvation and the forgiveness of sin would not be possible. Had we not humbled ourselves through repentance and faith, our reconciliation with God would not be possible.

Principle: Therefore, without humility, there can be no reconciliation.

Step 6 – Additional Reflections

When applying the Biblical text, one must remember the "put off/put on" principle described in Colossians chapter three. Just as nature abhors a vacuum, a Christian who "puts off" sin in the short-term but does not "put on" righteousness in the long-term will fill that void with sin. Therefore, as you construct your applications, be mindful of this principle. Furthermore, search the Scriptures for an individual who neglected to apply the principle. Reveal to the audience the consequence of disobedience. Also, search the Scriptures for an individual who employed the principle. Disclose to the audience the reward for obedience. These additional steps will confirm the application principle is biblically based and help the audience realize the importance and implications of embracing or neglecting these principles. Lastly, consider the various relationships and situations for this application. For example, could the scriptural principle be applicable in the following relationships: parent and child, husband and wife, employer and employee, co-workers, friends, strangers, or enemies?

APPLICATION

Psalm 103:1-5

Step 1 - Determine the application principle from the text

A. Primary Theme: Do not forget the Lord's benefits

B. Primary Subject: Believer

C. Actions: Don't forget

D. Outcome: Renewal

Step 2 - Choose the direction of the application principle

- Vertical – I should not forget God's benefits

Step 3 - Write out the application principle

- Remember to be Renewed

Step 4 - Confirm from Scripture the application principle

- **2 Corinthians 4:16–18** Therefore we do not

lose heart, but though our outer man is decaying, yet our inner man is being renewed day by day. For momentary, light affliction is producing for us an eternal weight of glory far beyond all comparison, while we look not at the things which are seen, but at the things which are not seen; for the things which are seen are temporal, but the things which are not seen are eternal.

Step 5 - Consider Illustrating the application principle

- Write out a brief story or illustration of this application principle.

Step 6 - Additional Reflections

- Write out your additional reflections

Matthew 8:23-27

Step 1 - Determine the application principle from the text

A. Primary Theme: Fear

B. Primary Subject: Disciples and Jesus

C. Actions: Storm, Fear, Miracle

D. Outcomes: calm storm and amazed disciples

Step 2 - Choose the direction of the application principle

- Vertical – Trust in Jesus when I am afraid

Step 3 - Write out the application principle

- Fearfulness is an opportunity to deepen your trust and understanding of God

Step 4 - Confirm from Scripture the application principle

- **Proverbs 29:25** The fear of man brings a snare, But he who trusts in the LORD will be exalted.
- **Philippians 1:12–14** Now I want you to know, brethren, that my circumstances have turned out for the greater progress of the gospel, 13 so that my imprisonment in the cause of Christ has become well known throughout the whole praetorian guard and to everyone else, 14 and

that most of the brethren, trusting in the Lord because of my imprisonment, have far more courage to speak the word of God without fear.

Step 5 - Consider Illustrating the application principle

- Write out a brief story or illustration of this application principle.

Step 6 - Additional Reflections

- Write out your additional reflections

PRESENTATION

- https://www.DigitalSword.org/application
- Download the application worksheet to guide your Bible study.
- Review the training videos to help you integrate the application into your message.

ELEMENTS OF APPLICATIONS

2 Timothy 4:2 (NASB95) — 2 preach the word; be ready in season and out of season; reprove, rebuke, exhort, with great patience and instruction.

Applications

1. Rooted in Scripture

2. Tangible expression of loving God and people

3. Christ-likeness
   - Pattern — Summarizing the attitudes and actions of people in the Bible
   - Principle — Summarizing the wisdom of Scriptural truths
   - Imperative — A clear command from the Biblical text

4. Direction
   - Vertical: God
   - Horizontal: People

5. Expression
   - Godly: How to behave
   - Worldly: How **not** to behave

6. Placement
   - Following the explanation
   - Concluding the message
   - Introducing the sermon

Figure 19. Elements of Application

SUMMARY

Goal

- To help believers glorify God by thinking, speaking, and acting like Christ.

Strategy

- Rooted in the foundation of proper Biblical interpretation, come alongside believers with practical help and guidance so they can apply the Wisdom of God to their lives.

Tactics/Assignments

- Choose a passage from the book of the Bible that you will be teaching and preaching
- Determine the single meaning of the passage and identify applications flowing from the Biblical text
- Determine the type of application: pattern, principle, imperative
- If applicable, discuss the implication of the application

Pitfalls & Warnings

- The number one pitfall is to call the audience to an application that is not rooted in the Biblical text

- The second pitfall is the failure to delineate between unbelievers and believers in the application
- The third pitfall is making the application so general that no change of life is required or so narrow it applies to no one
- The fourth pitfall is to create a man-centered application that focuses on human power and the flesh rather than a God-centered application relying on His power and the Spirit. Balance of both is required (Philippians 2:12-13)
- The fifth pitfall is to focus on short-term temporary change rather than the individual's long-term permanent change.
- The sixth pitfall is to wrongly prioritize God's kingdom's goals and the goals of men.
- The seventh pitfall is remaining in unconfessed sin and rebellion to God's word.
- The eighth pitfall is to strip from the application

the goal of Christlikeness and loving God and others.

EXCEL STILL MORE

- Did the exposition lay a biblical foundation for the application?
- Was the application placed correctly in the exposition?
- Is the application achievable?
- Did the application target the unbeliever or believer appropriately?
- Was there a good transition between the application and the Biblical text?
- Will the application result in Christlikeness and glorify God?
- Will the application require sacrificial love?
- Will the application achieve Kingdom goals?
- How will the application be achieved?

RECOMMENDED BOOKS

- Barton, Bruce, Philip Comfort, Grant Osborne, Linda K. Taylor, and Dave Veerman. *Life Application New Testament Commentary*. Wheaton, IL: Tyndale, 2001.
- Courson, Jon. *Jon Courson's Application Commentary*. Nashville, TN: Thomas Nelson, 2003.
- Doriani, Daniel M. *Putting the Truth to Work: The Theory and Practice of Biblical Application*. Phillipsburg, NJ: P&R Publishing, 2001.
- The *NIV Application Commentary*. Grand Rapids, MI: Zondervan Publishing House.
- Wilson, Neil S. *The Handbook of Bible Application*. Carol Stream, IL: Tyndale House Publishers, Inc., 2000.

CHAPTER ELEVEN

INGREDIENTS TO INGESTION: IS YOUR MESSAGE A MEAL, MORSEL, OR JUST EMPTY CALORIES?

"It is written, Man shall not live by bread alone, but by every word that proceedeth out of the mouth of God."

— Jesus the Word of God, Matthew 4:4

PURPOSE

Learn to evaluate your message and ensure it is Biblically substantive with theological depth.

PREPARATION

Your heart is pounding, your body is perspiring, and your mind is panicking! Words, ideas, images, and emotions are racing before your mind's eye. Pray. Breathe. Lift your eyes to the audience. Preach!

The preaching event that you have prepared for has arrived. There is no turning back. And like it or not, prepared or unprepared, you now stand before God, His people, and the lost as His mouthpiece.

Regardless of your giftedness, you will fall short. You cannot possibly live up to the perfect Word. There will always be a gap between what you know and how you live with what you know. However, this is not an excuse to engage in outright sin and rebellion, nor does it permit you to be passive to the temptations of this life. A preacher never stops endeavoring to be Christlike and holy. Pray for bi-vocational pastors because finding adequate time for them can be incredibly challenging.

The sermon is before you. The truths you have studied are coursing through your mind and heart. Strive to preach effectively. Seek to shepherd God's flock to Christlikeness, to love God and others, plead with them to obey God and His Word, and reach out to the lost.

Rely on the Holy Spirit to work in and through you and in and through those listening. Proclaim the Word of God boldly, fearing God and not man—trust in the power of God and the Word, and not in your persuasive communication skills. Be transparent and vulnerable, but not a victim nor needy. It's not about us, the preacher and teacher, but God and His flock.

As one preacher put it, "Invisible to men, there is a golden ball and chain from the Lord, attached to my life so that I remain at my post to study, preach, and serve Christ and His church." This imagery reflects the privilege, commitment, and hardship of a life dedicated to preaching the Word of God. So how does one become a better steward of preaching God's Word?

"Be diligent to present yourself approved to God as a workman who does not need to be ashamed, accurately handling the word of truth." (2 Timothy 2:15)

There is a plethora of literature on preaching discussing

the character of the preacher, conversations in the pulpit, creating flourishing churches, and converting the lost. One might think effective preaching is merely reading the right books and receiving the right teacher training. However, the stewardship of preaching is so much more than mere theory and training. For example, consider the preaching dynamics in three key areas: preparation, delivery, and response.

Each stage has multiple challenges and obstacles to overcome, which differ for each preacher and audience. How can we possibly grasp and communicate God's Word's full depth and breadth in our preparation? What is the best way to communicate intergenerationally and culturally? How can we overcome personal bias, errant thinking, and pride to hear and respond to God's revelation rightly? Do you comprehend the total weight and magnitude of preaching before a Holy God and His people? Do you keep the warning in James 3:1 afresh,

"Let not many of you become teachers, my brethren, knowing that as such we will incur a stricter judgment." Is it not truly an impossible task for the flesh alone? So, what must a preacher do? Preach Christ Crucified!

Look at the Old Testament, the New Testament, and the church's history, and you will discern that there will be seasons of joy and despair, fruit and fruitlessness, acceptance and persecution. But the man of God who denies himself, carries his cross, and faithfully follows Christ, and His word will bear fruit for the Kingdom. A Christ-centered mission and message is the only path of the preacher, "in season and out of season."

INSTRUCTION

So, what makes an exemplary sermon? There is a multitude of issues and factors to consider when preaching a message from God's word. We'll provide an expositional template and several sermon self-examination checklists to answer this question. But first, it is important to cover several concepts: elements of a proposition, five transition types, and several outline types.

The Proposition

A sermon without a purpose, are words for the wind!
—Anonymous

Have you (and most likely you have) listened to more than one sermon where you have no idea why the preacher preached the sermon? This is unfortunately an all-too-common occurrence. However, believe it or not, it is a very avoidable condition! It requires one simple step, the proposition statement.

The proposition is a one sentence, purpose statement. It describes for the audience what will be accomplished in the sermon. It will call them to act on the Biblical text. Without this purpose statement, the impact and power of the sermon is diminished. The sermon turns into a lecture rather than an exhortation for change! So, how do we build a proposition statement? Here is a helpful template, breaking down the essential elements.

Propositional Template
[# of Points in the Outline] + [Purpose Phrase] + [Reward, Punishment, Warning]

3 Parts of the Proposition

1) [# of Points in the Outline]
Overviews/Summarizes, Enumerates the key points of the message.

2) [Purpose Phrase]
Purpose Clause/Linking Clause/Transition Clause. It's a bridge to transition from the points of the message to the purpose of the message.

3) [Reward, Punishment, Warning]
Implication for obedience/reward and disobedience/punishment to God's Word, as well as warn to avoid a problem.

Example #1

Ephesians 2:1-10 Tonight, let's explore 3 foundational truths that will teach you and I how to live with the past and be transformed from "mess to masterpiece".

Breakdown

1) [# of Points in the Outline]
Ephesians 2:1-10 Tonight, let's explore 3 foundational truths

2) [Purpose Phrase]
that

3) [Reward, Punishment, Warning]
you and I how to live with the past and be transformed from "mess to masterpiece".

Explanation

The proposition tells us there will be a 3-point sermon and its implication is to help us live with the past in a transformative way. If we apply these 3 points, we will be transformed from "mess to masterpiece."

Example #2

From Psalm 103, David provides us with 5 critical steps in building a foundation to honor rather than dishonor God the Father in our worship.

Breakdown

1) [# of Points in the Outline]
From Psalm 103, David provides us with 5 critical steps in building a foundation

2) [Purpose Phrase]
to

3) [Reward, Punishment, Warning]
honor rather than dishonor God the Father in our worship.

Explanation

The proposition tells us this will be a 5-point sermon. If we apply these 5 points/steps, we will establish a foundation for a God-honoring life.

Example #3

Tonight, in Psalm 5, we will learn about 5 strategies when facing persecution so that our response will please our Lord and Savior Jesus Christ.

Breakdown

1) [# of Points in the Outline]
Tonight, in Psalm 5, we will learn about 5 strategies when facing persecution

2) [Purpose Phrase]
so that

3) [Reward, Punishment, Warning]
our response will please our Lord and Savior Jesus Christ.

Explanation

The proposition tells us this will be a 5-point sermon. If we apply these 5 points/strategies, we will discover way to obey and please the Lord Jesus Christ in difficult trials.

Final Thoughts

Can you see the elements more clearly now? Now you may be wondering, where should you place this "proposition"? I recommend you place it right at the end of the introduction and right before the body of the message. Lastly, I suggest restating and re-adjusting the proposition toward the end of the sermon.

The Transition

A sermon without proper transitions is like an intersection without stop lights! —Crash

One rainy night, on a dark road my car approached an intersection, and the lights were flashing yellow. It had been some time since my last road test…I thought to myself, does the flashing yellow light mean I stop or proceed? What about the other cars, will they stop?

Then I remembered, yellow means proceed with caution. So, I transitioned through the intersection safely, I saw the other lanes had a flashing red light, so they were stopped at the intersection, waiting for me to pass…safely!

Think with me about the many transitions in a sermon. There is a transition at the intersection between the introduction and the proposition. Next, we drive to the overview of the outline and then turn to the body of the message.

Within the body of the text, we motor through the explanation of the text, and then we see the illustrations, and pause at the application. Don't forget we need to venture further and bring our trip to an end with the conclusion.

Of course there might be other windy roads and unfamiliar landscapes as we add content as the Spirit leads. But remember, at each intersection, there must be some kind of transition, some kind of signpost to let your audience know where they are and where they are going.

As passengers in your "car," they are listening and wondering what the destination is, when will you stop, and what they should be watching on the journey. Because your sermon is "audio", they need "verbal signposts" or "verbal transitions" to assist them in navigating with you through your message.

So, what do these "verbal transitions" sound like? Here are my top five "verbal transition techniques":

1. Transition by Questioning
Sermon: *15 Words of Hope* by John MacArthur

At the beginning of paragraphs 7 and 8, he begins with a question and then proceeds to answer the question to transition from one paragraph to the next.

Example: But that brings up the question...**How**? The Apostle Paul has been talking about the ministry of reconciliation.

Note: The transition is the "How?" question placed between to other thoughts.

2. Transition by Summarizing

Sermon: *Jesus Christ and the Law of God* by John Piper

At the beginning of sermon, he uses this device to transition from the introduction to the body.

Example: I would like to **sum up** for you the meaning of Education for Exultation:
- **first**, the meaning as it relates to buildings;
- **second**, the meaning as it relates to funding;
- **third**, the meaning as it relates to process; and
- **fourth**, the meaning as it relates to Jesus Christ and

the Law of God.

Note: The transition is the summarizes all the key points.

3. Transition by Foreshadowing
Sermon: *The Ruler of the Waves* by J.C. Ryles

At the beginning of the introduction this preacher prepares our transition with clues as to what lies ahead in the next point.

Example: Come now, and let us study together a page in our Master's history. Let us consider what we may learn from the verses of Scripture which stand at the head of this tract. You see Jesus there crossing the lake of Galilee in a boat with his disciples. You see a sudden storm arise while He is asleep. The waves beat into the boat, and fill it. Death seems to be close at hand. The frightened disciples awake their Master and cry for help. He arises and rebukes the wind and waves, and at once there is a calm. He mildly reproves the faithless fears of his companions, and all is over. Such is the picture. It is one full of deep instruction. Come now and let us examine what we are meant to learn.

Note: All the elements will be explained in more detail that follows; the foreshadow provides a sneak peek.

4. Transition by Defining
Sermon: *Affliction is Certain* by Gil Rugh

Note how the preacher defines the word and transitions into an explanation.

Example: Paul says he prays for the Thessalonians "earnestly." **This word means "abundantly, beyond all measure, exceedingly, and overflowing all bounds."** It is an adverb that describes something that goes beyond all measure. So when Paul says that he is praying "earnestly," he is indicating the intensity with which he prays. This word is used only two other times in the New Testament, both times by Paul. In Ephesians 3:20, Paul says, "Now to Him who is able to do exceeding abundantly beyond all that we ask or think, according to the power that works within us." We cannot grasp, with our finite minds, all that God can do. It is "exceeding abundantly" all that we can comprehend. This is the same concept used in 1 Thessalonians 3:10. Paul is praying for them more than they could comprehend. His prayers for them are "overflowing." Do you have anyone in your life that you are praying for "earnestly?" Is it any wonder that Paul's ministry was effective?

Note: A concise definition is provided and then the details follow right into the message.

5. Transition by Bridging

AKA: "Peanut butter and jelly sandwich" or "Reese's peanut butter cup"

Sermon: *God's Handwriting Upon David* by Charles Spurgeon

This preacher simply takes two ideas, the one previous and the one next up and places it in one sentence.

Example: "And of the houses thereof," the **places where the priests and Levites dwelt**. Get a clear view **of the houses that Christ gives his people to dwell in**; how they dwell in him, how they abide in him, and go no more out for ever. I cannot enlarge on this; but you can think it out for yourselves, and explain it to your hearers and scholars. Think of those mansions of present joy and future bliss which they shall have who come in by the true and living way, even by Christ Jesus, who is the one way of entrance into the temple of salvation.

Note: Spurgeon mentions the houses of priest and Levites followed the mansions that Christ will provide. This is easiest and clearest of the transition to construct for the preacher and follow-along for the audience.

Websites

In wrapping up this topic, here are several websites that provide "transitional words and phrases":

1. http://owl.english.purdue.edu/owl/resource/574/02
2. http://www.uark.edu/campus-resources/qwrtcntr/resources/handouts/transitions.htm
3. http://www.smart-words.org/transition-words.html
4. http://www.ehow.com/how_4864740_use-transitional-devices.html
5. http://essays.org.uk/english/simplicity

Outline Types

In general, there are only two major types of Preaching/Teaching outlines: (1) Explanation and (1) Application. All other outlines combine these two basic forms.

The "Explanation Outline".

These outlines explain the text and depending on the detail, could very well stand alone and need no further explanation. These are the outlines you will find in most commentaries. Here is an example of the outline for Jude from the *Bible Knowledge Commentary*:

I. Salutation (vv. 1-2)

II. Warnings concerning Apostates (vv. 3-4)

III. Warnings concerning the Peril of Apostasy (vv. 5-16)

    A. Examples of apostates in the past (vv. 5-7)

        1. Egypt (v. 5)

        2. Angels (v. 6)

3. Sodom and Gomorrah (v. 7)

B. Actions of apostates in the present (vv. 8-16)

1. Rejecting authority (vv. 8-10)

2. Walking in error (v. 11)

3. Leading falsely (vv. 12-13)

4. Pleasing self (vv. 14-16)

IV. Guidelines for Avoiding Apostasy (vv. 17-23)

A. Remembering the teaching of the apostles (vv. 17-19)

B. Nurturing themselves (vv. 20-21)

C. Being merciful to others (vv. 22-23)

V. Victory over Apostasy (vv. 24-25)[1]

The "Application/Exhortation Outline". These outlines call you to respond to the text and require the preacher/teacher to connect the Biblical text to the application. Here is an "application" example

---

[1] John F. Walvoord, Roy B. Zuck and Dallas Theological Seminary, vol. 2, *The Bible Knowledge Commentary: An Exposition of the Scriptures* (Wheaton, IL: Victor Books, 1983-), 918-19. Logos Bible Software.

DIGITAL SWORD

modified from the *Life Application Bible Commentary:*

I. Beware of False Teachers (1–16)

II. Fight for God's truth (17–25)[2]

Now how do you choose between these two styles? First, always create the "explanation" outline first. This is the easiest to create, and should you later decide to create an "application" outline, you have a clearer understanding of the text and can properly connect the application to the text.

Improving Your Outline: Once you have chosen your outline type, consider ways to adjust your outline.

- **Alliteration** (Evangelize, Enroll, Educate)
- **Rhyme** (Pray, Obey, Stay, Stray) **This can come off as trite

---

[2] Bruce B. Barton, *1 Peter, 2 Peter, Jude*, Life application Bible commentary (Wheaton, Ill.: Tyndale House Pub., 1995), 233. Logos Bible Software.

- **All nouns** (The Man, The Cross, The Death, The Resurrection)
- **All verbs with progression** (Crawl, Walk, Run, Fly)
- **Proverbial / Principle** (Working Creates Wealth, Saving Supports Tomorrow, Giving to God Is a Form of Worship)
- **Chronological** (Day 1, Day 2, Day 3, Day 4, Day 5, Day 6)
- **Sentence** (As They Prayed, God Sent His Angel, And the Prisoner was set Free, And They Rejoiced)

Ways to Increase Engagement in Your Outline

- **Emotive vs. Cognitive:** Be aware of word choice. Abstract, intellectual cognitive words can bore, confuse and distance the speaker from the audience. Overly emotional can appear manipulative, exaggerated, and lacking substance. Find a good balance of both types of words.
- **Questions:** Asking questions is the quickest and

surest way to get the attention of the audience. Really good questions, can grab and hold attention.

- **Dilemma/Scenario:** Create a relatable situation with difficult choices can engage in audience in problem solving as well as challenge one decision making process.

- **Concise Illustration:** A brief imaginative or rooted in history story is a sure fire way to capture the attention of the audience.

- **Thought Provoking Statement:** Striking statements is a helpful way to arouse the attention of the audience. Be careful that it does not offend, or be too powerful it eclipses your point.

- **Keep the cookies Accessible:** Guard against providing raw exegetical data that is technical, full of jargon, and requires additional explanation. This will surely lose the attention of the audience.,

- **Principlization:** Providing a rule that can be applied in various situations can make the truth more applicable for more people and help others grow in their own thinking and application.

- **Application: Too Narrow vs Too General:** If an application is too narrow, no one in the audience will think it applies to them specifically. On the other hand, if the application is too general, they will presume they are already obeying and don't need to apply.

Attributes of an Effective Outline
- **Clear:** Easy to understand without an explanation.
- **Memorable**: Not too long or cumbersome to recall.
- **Reflective of the Biblical Text**: Rooted and grounded from sound exegesis of the Biblical text.
- **Logical/Rational**: Not requiring imagination or explanation. It almost seems like common sense.
- **Emotive**: Engages the audience, arouses interest, and commits them to journey through the text.
- **Structurally Consistent (linear, parallel):** There is an obvious pattern and flow to the outline.

- **Grammatically Consistent and Related** (all verbs, all past tense, etc.): The language is consistently used.

EXPOSITIONAL TEMPLATE

Preliminaries
- Title of the sermon
- Passage for preaching
- Time allotted for sermon
- Speaking rate (words per minute)
- Total words in the sermon

Introduction [time]
- Illustration / Application / Principle
- Purpose Statement introduced
- Outline Overview
- Transition

Point #1 [time]
- Engagement
- Explanation

- Exhortation
- Exit (transition)

Point #2 [time]
- Engagement
- Explanation
- Exhortation
- Exit (transition)

Point #3 [time]
- Engagement
- Explanation
- Exhortation
- Exit (transition)

Conclusion [time]
- Review outline
- Review the purpose statement in a concluding manner
- Final exhortation (illustration, application, principle)
- Prayer [time]

DIGITAL SWORD

Checklist #1: Examine Your Sermon

I. Purpose of Preacher

A. **Commanded:** 2 Timothy 4:1-5, 1 Timothy 4:13

B. **Model:** Ezra 7:10

- Set his heart/mind: Prepare/commit for the long view
- Study: Investigate
- Practice: To begin, maintain, and complete
- Teach: Disciple

C. The Character of the Preacher: Holy - Ephesians 3:5

D. A living reflection of the truth preached (1 Corinthians 9:27, 2 Timothy 2:20-26)

E. You are no more important than anyone else (1 Corinthians 3:5-15)

II. Purpose of the Audience

A. **To Receive the Word:** 1 Peter 2:1-3

B. **To Grow:** Ephesians 4:15

C. **To Serve:** Romans 12:1-2

D. **To Evangelize:** 2 Timothy 4:5, Jude 1:20-23, 2

Corinthians 5:20-21

III. Purpose of the Sermon: Transformation!

A. Truthful – Primarily Special Revelation, centered on the word (John 17:17)

B. Clear – Understandable to the saints (Matthew 28:18-20)

C. Exhortative – Call to obey, revealing the implication of the truth in their life (Acts 2:14, 38)

D. Exalt our God – He is on display, no one or no other thing (2 Corinthians 4:5)

E. Equip the Saints – Instruction is tied to the growth of the church (Ephesians 4:11-16)

F. Shepherd the Flock – they are sheep needing guidance and help (1 Peter 5:1-5)

G. Purpose of the Introduction
- Direct the audience's attention to God and His Word (as it is written...)
- Remove the audience's resistance to the speaker and the message (Romans 1:1)

- Ready the audience through curiosity and anticipation (Revelation 1:9-11)

H. Purpose of the Proposition

- Show the purpose and importance of the biblical message (Jude 1:3)
- Address the audience "Why should I care and listen about what you have to say? (Jude 1:4)

I. Purpose of the Outline

- Reflect on the major points of the Biblical Passage
- Organize what you will communicate about the passage from your study
- Guide the audience through the verbal experience
- Make it memorable
- Make it transferable/viral

J. Purpose of the Transition

- Show a separation of ideas: end your thought and begin a new thought

- Allow the audience the "catch-up" and/or take a mental/"audio break"
- To establish a pace through the passage

K. Purpose of the Exposition

- Explain the Biblical text for teaching, reproof, correction, and training (2 Tim 3:16-17, 2 Tim 2:14-17)
- Renew their mind (Romans 12:2, Ephesians 4:23)
- Make it Accessible to Build their life on the Word of God (Matthew 7:24-27)
- Warn (Ezekiel 3:17-21)

L. Purpose of the Illustration

- Support, Reinforce, and Point the audience to the Biblical Exposition
- *Play Second Fiddle:* Make the text more memorable than the illustration
- Rightly align the emotions of the audience to the atmosphere and emotion of the text

- Persuade, motivate, challenge, and charge but not manipulate
- Bridge the Biblical past with their present world

M. Purpose of the Application

- Support, Reinforce, and Point the audience to the Biblical Exposition
- *Play Second Fiddle:* Make the text more memorable than the illustration
- Rightly align the activities of the audience to the activities of the text
- Persuade, motivate, challenge, and charge but not manipulate
- Bridge the Biblical past with their present world

N. Purpose of the Conclusion

- Support, Reinforce, and Point the audience to the Biblical Exposition
- Make such an impact that the sermon will intersect their lives this week and beyond
- Finish what you started

- Review what has been said in a transferable/viral way

O. Purpose of the Emotion
- Support, Reinforce, and Point the audience to the Biblical Exposition
- Anchor and guide their emotions to the truth of the text
- Avoid just speaking to the intellect, but speak to their whole being
- Reflect the atmosphere and emotion of the text
- Humor: use it judiciously

P. Purpose of the Celebration
- Review the points of the sermon in a memorable fashion
- Take them to the cross in humility and thankfulness
- Take them to the resurrection for hope and power
- Equip them for the task of the Biblical text

Send them into the world as a holy servant, to be lights, witnesses, ambassadors, and evangelists

Q. The Church Environment
- The Church Service is primarily for believers! Preach to them!
- Recognize God is drawing some "unbelievers" for the truth
- Beware of "tares" and "hypocrites" and those that would do you harm
- Exalt God, Equip the Saints, Evangelize the Lost

R. "From Here to Eternity"
- Be responsible for the depth of your ministry, and let God be responsible for the breadth of your ministry
- Focus on the Right Reward (Matthew 6:19-20)

S. Body Language
- There were no nervous bodily movements or

distractions
- Movements of the body were intentional and appropriate
- Good eye contact
- Good posture

Checklist #2: Examine Your Sermon
- Outline (direction) of the sermon was clear and supportive of the proposition.
- Proposition
- Engaged the audience
- Displayed appropriate emotions
- Annunciation, Grammar, and Pronunciation
- Physical presence in the pulpit
- Demonstrated preparation for preaching
- Sermon reflected a logical flow
- Transitions maintained the flow of the sermon
- Sub-points supported the main points
- Gestures or speech habits that should be avoided
- Illustrations were strategically positioned and

effective in communicating biblical truth
- Application was derived from the text and relevant
- The conclusion brought the listener to the point of decision and supported the proposition
- Overall Strength and Weakness

Checklist #3: Examine Your Sermon

- The title summarizes the outline
- The outline summarizes the Biblical text
- The engagement introduces the exposition
- The exposition explains the Biblical text
- The exhortation illustrates and applies the Biblical text and flows from the exposition
- Examine your content
- Does it make the Biblical text clearer?
- Is it necessary?
- Do you have time?
- Where is the best place to position the content?
- Does the content flow directly from the

passage?

- Is the content organized logically?
- Do you have transitions at all the key places?
- Make sure the context of your cross-references connects appropriately to the Biblical text
- Is any content out of place or not related to the passage? Does it need to be moved or removed?
- Are you inserting "commercials" or "interruptions" in the flow of the explanation? (rabbit trails, unnecessary illustrations, etc.)
- Are you giving away the "end" at the "beginning"?
- Are you explaining content before citing the passage to be explained?
- Do you close succinctly and adequately with a single application or illustration?
- Are you "talking at" or "talking with" the

audience? Are you coming alongside the audience in the journey of discovering the truth of the text?

- Are you asking "implication questions" or creating "a real-life application scenario" so that the Biblical truth of the text being preached would be applied to avoid a crisis?
- Are you performing a speech, or are you delivering the truth?
- Are you sharing the convictions and passions that arose out of your study of the Biblical text?

Additional Thoughts

Study Communication Theory

- **Free:** http://2012books.lardbucket.org/books/a-primer-on-communication-studies/index.html
- **Fee:** http://www.amazon.com/gp/product/1577667069/ref=oh_details_o04_s00_i00?ie=UTF8&psc=1

Study Logic

- Geisler, Norman L., and Ronald M. Brooks. *Come, Let Us Reason: An Introduction to Logical Thinking.* Grand Rapids, MI: Baker Book House, 1990.
- Kindle, Free - Logic, Inductive, Deductive by William Minto
- Kindle, $10 – Logic by Isaac Watts

Study Rhetoric

- Aristotle. *Rhetoric, Translated by J. H. Freese.* Edited by J. H. Freese. Vol. 22. Medford, MA: Harvard University Press; William Heinemann Ltd., 1926.
- Dabney, Robert L. *Sacred Rhetoric: A Course of Lectures on Preaching.* Richmond, VA: Presbyterian Committee of Publication, 1870.
- Porter, Stanley E. Handbook of Classical Rhetoric in the Hellenistic Period, 330 B.C.-A.D. 400. Leiden; New York; Köln: Brill, 1997.

Checklist #4: Examine Your Sermon

Note: This form was utilized at the Master's Seminary

SERMON CRITIQUE SHEET

Evaluators Name ____________ Speaker's Name ____________

Class ____________ Box # ____________ Date ____________

Please evaluate the sermon, indicating whether you agree or disagree with these statements. Circle the number which best reflects your opinion. Additional comments will be helpful in order to provide specific feedback to the preacher.

5 Strongly Agree with the Statement
4 Agree with the Statement
3 Not Sure
2 Disagree with the Statement
1 Strongly Disagree with the Statement

Compared to other sermons I have heard I would grade this sermon as an A+ A A- B+ B B- C+ C C- D+ D D- F because

Introduction	The introduction gained my attention	5	4	3	2	1
	The introduction related well to the sermon's proposition	5	4	3	2	1
	The introduction was linked to the experiences of the audience	5	4	3	2	1
	The audience was immediately drawn into the message	5	4	3	2	1
	Comments					

Proposition	The Proposition was obvious and clearly stated	5	4	3	2	1
	The Proposition was identified early in the message	5	4	3	2	1
	Comments					

Transition	The transitions tied the main parts of the sermon together	5	4	3	2	1
	The transitions connected the main points of the sermon outline	5	4	3	2	1
	The transitions were smooth and not to obvious	5	4	3	2	1
	Comments					

Sermon Outline	The outline clearly unfolded and supported the proposition	5	4	3	2	1
	The outline clearly followed a logical progression	5	4	3	2	1
	The outline was consistent with the content	5	4	3	2	1
	A listener could easily identify the outline	5	4	3	2	1
	Main points supported the proposition	5	4	3	2	1
	Sub points clearly related to the main point	5	4	3	2	1
	Comments					

Content	The sermon was built on solid exegesis	5	4	3	2	1
	The speaker knew his passage well	5	4	3	2	1
	The speaker's message was theologically and doctrinally sound	5	4	3	2	1
	New scriptural insights were revealed	5	4	3	2	1
	The meaning of the text was explained clearly	5	4	3	2	1
	The speaker did not take the passage out of context	5	4	3	2	1
	There was a clear application of biblical truth to the listener's life	5	4	3	2	1
	The speaker made a reference to the gospel	5	4	3	2	1
	The sermon sufficiently emphasized the greatness of Christ	5	4	3	2	1
	Comments					

Figure 20. Master's Seminary Sermon Critique Sheet

INGREDIENTS TO INGESTION

		5	4	3	2	1
Conclusion	The conclusion summarized the proposition in a new way	5	4	3	2	1
	The conclusion was stated concretely	5	4	3	2	1
	The conclusion was stated in a positive manner	5	4	3	2	1
	The conclusion brought the listener to a personal response	5	4	3	2	1
	The conclusion motivated the hearer to know, love or serve God more	5	4	3	2	1
	Comments					
Illustrations	The illustrations illumined the point being made	5	4	3	2	1
	The illustrations captured the listeners attention	5	4	3	2	1
	The audience could identify with the illustrations	5	4	3	2	1
	The speaker did not drag out illustrations unnecessarily	5	4	3	2	1
	Illustrations from Scripture were accurate	5	4	3	2	1
	Illustrations were woven nicely into the message	5	4	3	2	1
	Comments					
Body Language	Facial expressions conveyed urgency	5	4	3	2	1
	The speaker maintained direct eye contact with listeners	5	4	3	2	1
	The preacher had good posture	5	4	3	2	1
	His gestures were meaningful and definite	5	4	3	2	1
	He did not show any distracting nervous habits	5	4	3	2	1
	Comments					
Communication	The speaker used good grammar	5	4	3	2	1
	His voice was strong and loud enough	5	4	3	2	1
	The speaker showed vocal variety	5	4	3	2	1
	The preacher used good diction	5	4	3	2	1
	He read the biblical text with enthusiasm	5	4	3	2	1
	He used contemporary language his audience could understand & defined terms	5	4	3	2	1
	There was a clear application of biblical truth to the listener's life	5	4	3	2	1
	The speaker made reference to the gospel	5	4	3	2	1
	The sermon sufficiently emphasized the greatness of Christ	5	4	3	2	1
	Comments					
Delivery	The speaker seemed well prepared	5	4	3	2	1
	The delivery of his sermon demonstrated self confidence	5	4	3	2	1
	The speaker drew me into his message with passion	5	4	3	2	1
	In general, he communicated well with his audience	5	4	3	2	1
	I learned something new	5	4	3	2	1
	The preacher desired to be heard	5	4	3	2	1
	The speaker maintained my interest throughout the message	5	4	3	2	1
	I had the impression the speaker truly cared about me	5	4	3	2	1
	The sermon spoke to some of my personal needs	5	4	3	2	1
	Comments					

Figure 21. Master's Seminary Sermon Critique Sheet

APPLICATION

- Take a recent sermon and self-evaluate with the forms above. Additionally, select several trusted individuals and have them complete the analysis.

PRESENTATION

- https://www.DigitalSword.org/review
- Download the self-analysis worksheet to guide your Bible study

SUMMARY

Goal

- To arrange the sermon for optimal clarity and Biblical accuracy for glorifying God, edifying and maturing the saints, and guiding the lost to Christ.

Strategy

- Cultivate and expand your giftedness as a teacher and preacher.
- Review the rules of excellent verbal communication.
- Arrange the sermon to guide the audience into the Biblical truth in an engaging manner.

- Help your audience to gain a deeper understanding of the Biblical text.
- Lead them with the help of the Holy Spirit to be transformed by the Scriptures.

Tactics

- Choose a passage from the book of the Bible that you will be teaching and preaching
- Arrange your sermon in the following manner
- Convert the raw exposition portion of your sermon into preachable material appropriate for the audience.
- Integrate the word studies and grammatical insights, historical and theological background, cross-references, and commentaries insights into a logical, rational, compelling, and engaging format reflecting the author's intended meaning.
- Create and refine the propositional statement
- Arrange the placement of the illustrations and applications

- Create transitional statements
- Complete your conclusion
- Appropriately call the audience to understand the text and take Biblical action rightly
- Utilize an illustration, application, principle, etc.
- Complete the introduction
- Appropriately get the audience's attention, driving interest in the message of the Biblical text
- Complete the final outline
- Read aloud, practicing the presentation, correcting the sermon's flow, logic, sentence length, transition, and anything that would hinder clarity and accuracy

Pitfalls & Warnings

- The number one pitfall is not to pray for your audience and yourself
- The second pitfall is to rely on your flesh and not the Spirit

- The third pitfall is not re-reading the sermon
- The fourth pitfall is not having clear transitions between points
- The fifth pitfall is not walking through the sermon aloud at least once
- The sixth pitfall is waiting until the last minute to complete the sermon
- The seventh pitfall is not to rest before the sermon
- The eighth pitfall is not having variety in your sermons week to week
- The ninth pitfall is not planning ahead in your preaching schedule
- The tenth pitfall is to conform your preaching to another style rather than cultivating your own individuality and giftedness
- The eleventh pitfall is not to cultivate holiness and confession of sin and application of the Biblical truth being studied and preached

- The twelfth pitfall is not being willing to evaluate your sermons and identify weaknesses and areas of improvement so that you become more skilled at preaching God's Word

EXCEL STILL MORE

- Did the sermon opening engage?
- Was the proposition stated, clearly understood, and fulfilled in the sermon?
- Did the outline reflect the text, engage the audience, and make the Biblical text more memorable?
- Was the sermon logical, emotive, and clear?
- Was there a proper placement of illustrations, applications, and cross-references, and were they rightly related to the Biblical text?
- Were relevant historical and theological elements appropriately placed in the sermon, communicated to the audience, and rightly connected to the Biblical text?

- Was the exegesis and explanation of the text rightly related to the audience?
- Were transitions employed and effectively used?
- Were there any doctrinal or factual errors?
- How much eye contact?
- Any significant verbal or body language concerns?
- Was humor appropriately utilized?
- How was the overall emotional tone?
- Was the speaker authentic, genuine, transparent, and credible?
- Did the sermon close properly?

RECOMMENDED BOOKS

NOTE: The following is a list of specific resources that have improved my preaching.

- Alcántara, Jared E. *Crossover Preaching.* Westmont, IL: IVP Academic, 2015.
- Anderson, Kenton C. *Choosing to Preach: A*

Comprehensive Introduction to Sermon Options and Structures. Grand Rapids, MI: Zondervan Publishing House, 2006.

- Atkinson, Max. *Lend Me Your Ears: All You Need to Know about Making Speeches and Presentations*. Oxford University Press, 2004.
- Carter, Terry G., J. Scott Duvall, and J. Daniel Hays. *Preaching God's Word*. Grand Rapids, MI: Zondervan, 2005.
- McDill, Wayne. *12 Essential Skills for Great Preaching: Second Edition, Revised and Expanded*. Nashville, TN: B&H Publishing Group, 2006.
- Chapell, Bryan. *Christ-Centered Preaching: Redeeming the Expository Sermon*. Third Edition. Grand Rapids, MI: Baker Academic: A Division of Baker Publishing Group, 2018.
- Craddock, Fred B., and Thomas G. Long. *Preaching*. Nashville: Abingdon Press, 2010.

- Hughes, Jack. *Expository Preaching with Word Pictures*. Scotland, UK: Christian Focus, 2014.
- Kistler, Don, ed. *Feed My Sheep: A Passionate Plea for Preaching*. Lake Mary, FL: Reformation Trust Publishing, 2008.
- Lloyd-Jones, D. Martyn. *Preaching And Preachers: 40th Anniversary Edition*. Zondervan, 2012.
- MacArthur, John F., Jr. *MacArthur Pastor's Library on Preaching*. Nashville, TN: Thomas Nelson Publishers, 2005.
- Miller, Calvin. *Preaching: The Art of Narrative Exposition*. Grand Rapids, MI: Baker Books, 2006.
- Reid, Robert Stephen. *The Four Voices of Preaching*. Grand Rapids, MI: Brazos Press, 2006.
- Richard, Ramesh. *Preparing Expository Sermons: A Seven-Step Method for Biblical*

Preaching. Grand Rapids, MI: Baker Books, 2001.

- Robinson, Haddon W. *Biblical Preaching: The Development and Delivery of Expository Messages*. Third. Grand Rapids, MI: Baker Academic, 2014.

- Vines, Jerry, and Jim Shaddix. *Power in the Pulpit: How to Prepare and Deliver Expository Sermons*. Chicago, IL: Moody Press, 1999.

- York, Hershael W., and Bert Decker. *Preaching with Bold Assurance: A Solid and Enduring Approach to Engaging Exposition*. Nashville, TN: Broadman & Holman Publishers, 2003.

CHAPTER TWELVE

TICKLING EARS TO TRAINING HEARTS: WHAT KIND OF MESSAGE ARE YOU COMMUNICATING?

"For the time will come when they will not endure sound doctrine; but after their own lusts shall they heap to themselves teachers, having itching ears; And they shall turn away their ears from the truth, and shall be turned unto fables."

— Paul the Apostle, 2 Timothy 4:3-4

PURPOSE

Learn the procedures as well as the pitfalls in creating a topical message.

PREPARATION

Have you experienced a topical sermon that was encouraging, riveting, and life-changing but devoid of the Scriptures? Let me set the record straight; that is not a topical sermon…that is a motivational speech!

One of the most treacherous preaching paths you can navigate is preparing a topical sermon. A topical message is an excellent complement to the expository sermon. A healthy balance of these two sermonic approaches is critical for contemporary audiences to balance truth and application.

When it comes to the topical message, it is easy to veer off course, neglecting Scripture as the source of wisdom to form a message of man's wisdom, appealing to what is popular and practical, feeding the flesh, and meeting the audience's felt needs. A sermon must be engaging, relevant, and helpful, but it must do so by being anchored to the truths of the Biblical text. The age in which we live has many gurus, self-help experts, motivational speakers, and blogging experts preaching worldly wisdom. Will you join their chorus, or will you be like wisdom personified by Proverbs 2, crying aloud in the streets?

Through her preachers, teachers, and evangelists, the Church's calling is to proclaim God's Word and His

Wisdom to exalt God, edify the body of Christ and evangelize the world. We desperately need the kind of discernment which flows from a thorough study of the Bible and a lifelong pursuit and application of Christ's word in holiness, humility, confession of sin, and service. Certain secular wisdom is beneficial, may even be generally rooted and related to Biblical truths, and may have a place in the believer's life. However, the challenge before us is not to be worldly-wise but Word-wise, skillful in understanding God's Word and applying the Scriptures practically to our lives in all situations in our sojourning. The topical sermon is excellent for showing people how to think and act Biblically.

These subject-based messages are an excellent format for a particular church event or a discipleship series to address practical issues in the local church. The topical sermon is also a helpful way to break up the verse-by-verse monotony many teachers and preachers fall into with their preaching ministries. Additionally, a succession of topical sermons may be inserted strategically during a more extended expository series when appropriately planned. This strategy is optimal and preferred, resulting in more time for application. I wholeheartedly recommend this approach! Preach 3-5 weeks verse by verse, and then preach a topic flowing from the exposited text for 1-2 weeks. Just be sure the topic flows from the most recent passages preached. For example, let's say you are teaching through Mark's Gospel, and you come to the passage where Jesus discusses divorce. Why not, at this point, break into a topical series on marriage? This opportunity will allow you to go more in-depth on the topic, bring greater depth to the issue, and address the audience's needs. This kind of preaching is exciting, refreshing, and immensely practical.

As you consider preaching topically, let me caution you

with the following advice. Master first, the topical exposition. These messages focus on a single topic and aggregate all the vital related passages to this topic. A simple way to get started is with a topical Bible like *Naves Topical Bible*. Discover the definitive or critical text for the issue you are studying. Then, identify the most relevant related Biblical subtopics and their corresponding passages. Arrange the topical sermon so the audience can think Biblically and then act on those Biblical truths for their particular situation. One way to arrange a topic message is chronological, starting with the Old Testament and ending with the New Testament. Another option is to commence with the 'general' and then move to the 'specific.' Avoid topics where the Scriptures are silent and issues that rely too much on the world's wisdom and personal experience. Choose topics that your audience desperately needs Biblical knowledge and understanding. Seek to resolve the problems people are currently facing with Biblical solutions. Encourage them in their fight and struggle against sin. Provide wisdom for repairing and restoring broken relationships.

The topical sermon should be inspiring, encouraging, immensely practical, and foremost Biblical! Don't shy away from controversy, but handle it as wise statesmen. Be candid, but remember, "Let your speech always be with grace, seasoned with salt, that you may know how you ought to answer each one." (Colossians 4:6). Allow the Word to do its work, as Paul wrote in 2 Timothy 4:2, "Preach the word! Be ready in season and out of season. Convince, rebuke, exhort, with all longsuffering and teaching." And remember, the topical sermon is just one of many preaching tools to equip the body of Christ, providing discernment and wisdom for the troubled times in which we live.

INSTRUCTION

The following strategies will guide you in forming a topical exposition whereby the application will flow appropriately from the Biblical text.

Steps for Building Topic Exposition

We will illustrate these steps with the topic of humility.

Step 1 - Selecting the Topic that is Rooted in the Scriptures

There are two primary ways by which to select a topic for exposition. The first method is to locate a topic-based resource, such as *Nave's Topical Bible*, *Nelson's Topical Bible Index*, *MacArthur's Topical Bible*, or *Where to Find it in the Bible*. For our example, we will utilize *Nelson's Topical Bible Index*. These resources list the topics alphabetically, so finding your subject is relatively straightforward. Additionally, the resource provides a basic outline for organizing the material into subtopics. This layout is beneficial for outlining and choosing the best passages related to the topic. *Nelson's*

Topical Bible Index for the subject of humility provides thirty-seven scriptural references organized into five categories: (1) factors involved in the sense of, (2) factors producing, (3) rewards of, (4) Christians exhorted to, and (5) Examples of.

The second method is to utilize Bible software to identify topics related to a passage of Scripture. Utilizing the 'Topic Bible Reference Guide' in Logos Bible Software for Philippians 2:8, the guide resulted in over 80 related topics. Some of the topic results included: humility, the humility of Jesus, Christian attributes, abasement, the meekness of Jesus, self-denial, and unselfishness. In Logos, choosing the topic 'humility' locates resources that include topical Bibles, Bible dictionaries, and encyclopedias, all of which provide additional subtopics, commentary, and Bible cross-references.

Whether you begin with the topic that leads to Scripture or Scripture that leads to a topic, either path is valid as long as the Scriptures drive the topic. Guard against creating a topic where you organize verses based on personal preference rather than theology. Once you have a list of cross-references, you are ready for the next step.

Step 2 - Choosing the Key Biblical Passages

With our topic of 'humility' selected, we are now ready to choose and prioritize Scripture. Selecting the right Scriptures can be difficult, so let me provide several guidelines.

DIGITAL SWORD

A. Locate the clearest passages on the topic that speak primarily about the subject matter and nothing else.

B. Look for passages that illustrate the topic through a person, place, action, or event.

C. Find passages that connect the main topic to a subtopic in a clear, direct way—for example, humility and prayer or humility and joy.

D. Discover Scriptures that reveal a reward for obedience or consequence for disobedience related to your topic.

E. Seek the wisdom literature (Psalms, Job, Proverbs, Ecclesiastes) for principles, proverbial sayings, and illustrations that may be helpful for application.

As you choose Scripture, ensure that each passage is not repeating the topical idea but is expanding, illustrating, and applying the topic in new and different ways. This approach will prevent the topic from being flat and lacking variety.

Step 3 - Checking your Biblical Counseling Resources

Another resource to investigate for a topical exposition is counseling resources. These books are beneficial for identifying Scriptures and their related applications. Additionally, they provide a framework in their discussions to ensure you are not merely focusing on external behavior but also examining one's heart and personal motivations. Since a topical exposition aims to explain the Scripture and apply the text to the listener's mind and heart, counseling resources are an excellent resource to consult in this endeavor. One particular resource that is quite helpful in providing Scriptures, topical outlines, and related subjects is the June Hunt's *Hope for the Heart Biblical Counseling Library*. This resource covers an extensive number of practical topics, all tied to specific Scriptures.

Step 4 - Thinking about the Theological Implications

As you seek to explain and apply the Scriptures, you must be theologically precise, understand related theological issues, and be aware of theological implications. For example, the practice of asceticism, whereby one denies themselves through excessive fasting and other austere practices, can appear humble when it is an external work of fleshly pride.

Step 5 - Forming the Final Outline

I. Humility: Christ's Example (Phil. 2:5–11)
A. Attitude

B. Action

C. Adoration

II. Humility: Church's Expression (Eph. 4:1–3)
A. Attitude

B. Action

C. Affection

Step 6 - Concluding the Message

Principle: Without humility, there can be no

reconciliation

Step 7 – Reviewing the Topical Exposition

Review all the cross-references and their corresponding contexts to ensure you are not taking a verse out of its context and misapplying it. Avoid proof-texting at all costs!

APPLICATION

Below you will find several topical sermons. As you read or listen, please notice how the topic and scriptures are organized.

- Heaven Topical Series: John MacArthur
    - https://www.gty.org/library/topical-series-library/175/heaven
- John Patton (Christian Biography): John Piper
    - https://www.desiringgod.org/messages/you-will-be-eaten-by-cannibals-lessons-from-the-life-of-john-g-paton
- Justice of God: Tim Keller
    - https://gospelinlife.com/downloads/the-justice-of-god-4925/

- Sinners in the Hands of an Angry God: Jonathan Edwards
  - https://www.blueletterbible.org/Comm/edwards_jonathan/Sermons/Sinners.cfm
- Walking with God: George Whitefield
  - https://www.ccel.org/ccel/whitefield/sermons.iv.html
- David's Dying Prayer: Charles Spurgeon
  - http://www.romans45.org/spurgeon/sermons/0129.htm
- Shocking Youth Message: Paul Washer
  - https://www.sermonaudio.com/sermoninfo.asp?SID=52906154239

PRESENTATION

- https://www.DigitalSword.org/topical
- Download the topical worksheet to guide your Bible study.
- Review the training videos to help you create a topical outline as you study with your computer.

SUMMARY

Goal

- To preach a topical sermon flowing from the Biblical text rather than flowing from man's wisdom.

Strategy

- To derive a topic from the Biblical text and determine the essential Biblical passage(s) to allow God's Word to address the topic.

Tactics

- Choose a topic and find the critical passage from which the Bible provides insight, illumination, explanation, and application
- Identify the key related subtopics and corresponding Biblical passages
- Determine the topic template to arrange the message in an orderly fashion
- Using your topical bibles, thematic resources, dictionaries, and encyclopedias, be sure to check

your work to make sure you have the key ideas expressed
- Make sure you have not overlooked the needs of your audience in the various topics you have identified
- Locate any books that are exclusively devoted to your subject matter and review them to ensure you are examining the subject from multiple perspectives, even those that you may disagree with doctrinally
- Look for applications and life principles that flow from the Bible passages related to the topic
- Ensure the topic, insights, and applications are relevant to your audience
- Consult Biblical counseling resources to find additional applications

Pitfalls & Warnings
- The number one pitfall is to choose a topic and not allow the Bible to speak on the topic

- The second pitfall is picking a passage for the topical sermon and never explaining the passage
- The third pitfall is choosing a topic that has nothing to do with the Bible
- The fourth pitfall is choosing subtopics utterly unrelated to the main topic
- The fifth pitfall is to choose subtopics that are Biblical but not the most important topics
- The sixth pitfall is leaving out applications
- The seventh pitfall is not bridging the Bible to the audience
- The eighth pitfall is to draw too much or center on personal experience
- The ninth pitfall is to make the topic so practical there is no theological thrust.
- The tenth pitfall is to make the topic so man-centered that the topical sermon becomes more about "Me" than "God."

EXCEL STILL MORE

- What was the key Bible passage for the topic?
- Which was more prominent and passionate, the Bible or personal experience and personal wisdom?
- Were the subtopics rooted in the Biblical text?
- Were the subtopics the most significant subtopics related to the topic?
- Were there any missing, significant subtopics that should have been mentioned?
- Were there any subtopics that could have been left out and avoided?
- Were all the subtopics rightly related and prioritized in the sermon?
- Was this topic relevant and practical?
- Did the topical sermon have a theological thrust or emphasis on knowing God and His Word?
- Was there a call to holiness?
- Did the topical sermon have a man-centered

emphasis or a God-centered emphasis?

RECOMMENDED BOOKS

- Anderson, Ken. *Where to Find It in the Bible.* Nashville: T. Nelson Publishers, 1996.
- Burkett, Larry. *The Word on Finances.* Chicago: Moody Publishers, 1994.
- Chan, Sam, and Malcolm Gill. *Topical Preaching in a Complex World: How to Proclaim Truth and Relevance at the Same Time.* Grand Rapids, MI: Zondervan Academic, 2021.
- Davis, Barry L. *52 Topical Sermons.* Vol. 1. Pulpit Outlines Series. Barry Davis, 2013.
- Davis, Barry L. *52 Topical Sermons.* Vol. 2. Pulpit Outlines Series. Barry Davis, 2013.
- Davis, Barry L. *52 Topical Sermons.* Vol. 3. Pulpit Outlines Series. Barry Davis, 2013.
- Davis, Barry L. *52 Topical Sermons.* Vol. 4. Pulpit Outlines Series. Barry Davis, 2013.

- Ehorn, Seth, and Linda Washington. *The A to Z Guide to Finding It in the Bible: A Quick-Scripture Reference.* Grand Rapids, MI: Baker Books, 2010.
- Elwell, Walter A., and Douglas Buckwalter. *Topical Analysis of the Bible: With the New International Version.* Vol. 5. Baker Reference Library. Grand Rapids, MI: Baker Book House, 1996.
- McCordic, Charles W. *The Thematic Bible: Topical Analysis.* Bellingham, WA: Logos Bible Software, 2007.
- Miller, Daniel Morrison, and Geoffrey Stonier, eds. *The New Thematic Concordance.* Ross-shire, Scotland: Christian Focus Publications, 2005.
- Ridolfi, Brian. *What Does the Bible Say About...: The Ultimate Bible Answer Book.* WORDsearch, 2006.

- Swanson, James, and Orville Nave. *New Nave's Topical Bible*. Oak Harbor: Logos Research Systems, 1994.
- Thomas Nelson Publishers. *Find It Fast in the Bible*. Nashville: T. Nelson Publishers, 2000.
- Thomas Nelson Publishers. *Nelson's Quick Reference Topical Bible Index*. Nelson's Quick Reference. Nashville, TN: Thomas Nelson Publishers, 1996.
- Thompson, Frank Charles. *Thompson Chain Reference Bible: Topical Index*. Kirkbride Bible Company, 1997.
- Torrey, R.A. *The New Topical Text Book: A Scriptural Text Book for the Use of Ministers, Teachers, and All Christian Workers*. Oak Harbor, WA: Logos Bible Software, 2001.
- Vaughan, Kenelm. *The Divine Armory of Holy Scripture*. The American Edition Revised. Public Domain: Catholic Book Exchange, 1894.

- Wiersbe, Warren W. *Index of Biblical Images: Similes, Metaphors, and Symbols in Scripture*. Grand Rapids, MI: Baker Books, 2000.

CHAPTER THIRTEEN

A ROSE BY ANY OTHER NAME WOULD SMELL AS SWEET!

"And a certain Jew named Apollos, born at Alexandria, an eloquent man, and mighty in the Scriptures, came to Ephesus."

— Luke the Physician, Acts 18:24

PURPOSE

Learn to expand your sermon preparation and delivery skill sets in five key areas to better communicate to a broader audience for more effective preaching and teaching.

INSTRUCTION

There are many areas of consideration for improving your ability to develop a message and communicate God's Word. Each preacher and teacher have varying strengths, weaknesses, and giftedness, as well as different personalities and experiences. Therefore, as you study this chapter, identify your present range of skills but also see where you can grow and venture into new preaching territories. These incremental changes will help you expand your range of abilities and improve your skill sets. Your audience will especially appreciate your growth and not using the same repetitive preaching style each week.

The five central areas we will explore in this chapter include the following: Content, Construction, Collection, Communication, and Connection. Let me define each of these in more detail.

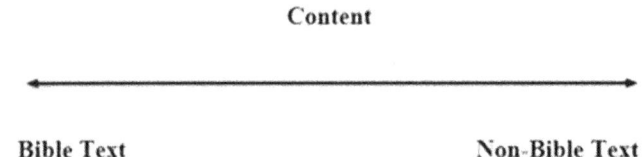

1. Content

This first category is the most important since it is the source and substance of your message. The spectrum of your sermon will range from Biblical text to non-biblical text. Learning how to evaluate whether your message is truly centered on God's Word or man's wisdom is important. Do not deceive yourself and think that because your sermon explains a passage, it's necessarily a substantive Biblical message. I have sat under preachers who will read a passage, gloss over its meaning in a superficial way, and then fill most of their sermon with the non-biblical text of stories, illustrations, etc., thinking they have exposited the Biblical text.

Let's not confuse the issue; spiritual truth and spiritual power reside in God's word, not one's personal anecdotes. Although stories and illustrations can make a personal connection and help one connect to the truth and the Savior, your personal experience is not inspired. It cannot replace the expositing of God's word. When you rely too much on stories and illustrations, you shift the audience's dependence from the Holy Spirit to you and from God's Word to your 'wisdom.' That is unholy usurpation.

So how do you guard against such a fatal move for you and your audience? Examine your motive. Do the hard work of deep study. Review your message and see where the truth is primarily anchored and explained. If you're presenting the truth primarily through stories and illustrations rather than Biblical reasoning with word studies, grammar, biblical cross-references, historical and theological backgrounds, biblical illustrations, and applications, then your message fails the test of Biblical substance and content.

A word of caution. Stories, illustrations, and applications can be rooted in Scripture, so do not think that I am suggesting these are inappropriate or only to be used as a last resort. Let's not throw out the baby with the bath water! When crafting your message, one needs to step back and ask whether the overall content of the message is God and word-centered or man-centered. This analysis cannot be purely the number of Scriptures quoted or explained. One must consider the arguments, illustrations, applications, transitions, and overall ideas conveyed. For example, a message could be very Biblical but dead and dry. On the other hand, a sermon could be engaging and illuminating, but it's merely stories and the wisdom of men.

Don't be lazy filling the preaching time with poor substitutes for actual biblical truth. Charles Spurgeon was a master at pithy sayings, stories, and illustrations that did not distract nor direct his audience away from the Biblical truth. On the contrary, he redirected and anchored them to the Bible and the Savior, Jesus Christ. There is a difference! Though it can be subtle at times, it matters. Have a heart-to-heart prayer time with the Lord reviewing your sermon content. Seek His face and be committed to proclaiming Him and His Word in His Church.

DIGITAL SWORD

Exercise

Take one of your recent sermons with two highlighter pens of two different colors. Every time you clearly reference the Bible or biblical ideas, highlight this text with one color. Then with a different color, highlight your stories, applications, personal anecdotes, and any other material like your transitions, introductions, arguments, exhortations, and conclusions that lack Biblical substance. Your message should be approximately 80 percent biblical substantive and 20 percent non-Bible. How did your sermon fair? What needs to change in your sermon to be more Biblical?

Construction

⬅———————————————➡

Exposition   **Narrative**

2. Construction

The second category is construction. Here one must choose a preaching structure for the message. One of the finest books that define the major preaching structures is *Choosing to Preach: A Comprehensive Introduction to Sermon Options and Structures* by Kenton Anderson. The author puts forth four primary structures: declarative, pragmatic, narrative, and visionary. The author then suggests a fifth structure, a composite of the previous four mentioned. Every sermon will touch upon one or more of these structures. Choosing a structure is never done in a vacuum but rather should be driven first by the structure of the Biblical text and second by that which best supports the exposition and application of His truth. Each structure has strengths and weaknesses, and each structure can communicate truth effectively if appropriately applied. Therefore, one should become familiar with these structures and, as the author Kenton Anderson suggests, learn to integrate them effectively to communicate the truth of God's Word clearly.

A bit of caution here. First, remember the structure itself is not what makes a great sermon; it's the clarity of the truth conveyed. Second, don't try to implement a whole new structure in your sermon but incrementally experiment with other structural forms in part within the sermon. Third, ensure your sermon reflects the structure of the text as much as possible. For example, when the surprise point comes at the end, ensure your message does not give away the surprise at the beginning. If the text is a story, continue that form in your preaching as well, but leave some room to break from the structure when necessary. Fourth, don't rely on one structure all the time, but vary when possible and make good sense. Don't sacrifice clarity on the altar of cleverness.

Exercise

Review ten of your sermons using Kenton Anderson's *Choosing to Preach* to identify the various structures utilized in your sermons and then identify the predominant structure. Then list the structures you will begin to integrate into your future sermons. Be intentional but incremental.

Collection

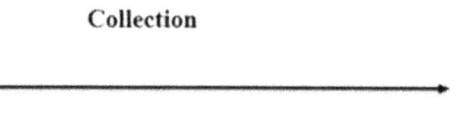

Memory   **Manuscript**

3. Collection

Our third category is the collection which refers to how you will write and organize your final message to preach. The superior method is noteless with extemporaneous delivery. If you have the memory skills or can rehearse and practice your message so that you can stand before your audience without any or few little notes and helps and still convey the message directly, passionately, and accurately, then you are most fortunate! But the rest of us will need to rely on some help, whether a simple outline, detailed outline, extensive notes, or a full manuscript.

The goal should be to remove total dependency on a manuscript without giving up precision and detail. However, if you rely on a manuscript, consider practicing before you preach and teach to make more eye contact and be more conversational. Discover how many "practice out loud" or "read aloud through the sermon sessions" you need to be comfortable with the manuscript and make excellent eye contact. Be sure to add that time for rehearsal so that you arrive at the pulpit prepared.

One last thought. Regardless of the notes you bring into the pulpit, strive to speak to the audience directly without any notes at strategic times. Be intentional in planning for these moments, particularly when exhorting, encouraging, making applications, having intimate moments with the audience, and making significant theological points.

Exercise

Identify three to five places in your sermon where you can go noteless. Then, for the following ten sermons you will preach, attempt to connect with your audience without notes in those selected portions. If necessary, rehearse and memorize, but leave room for the Holy Spirit within you to go off script when necessary.

Communication

◄─────────────────────────────────────►

Lecture   **Conversation**

4. Communication

Communication is the fourth category and addresses your fundamental view of the audience and how you wish to interact with them. Ask yourself the following questions. First, are you above, equal, or below the audience before God? In other words, positionally in Christ, are you equal or not with them before the Lord? This is a key attitudinal question. Second, as a gifted preacher and teacher in authority spiritually, is the congregation there to serve you, or are you there to serve them? Third, do you see the need to vary your interactions based on the nature of the message and the passage's difficulty, accommodating for the needs in the body? Fourth, how much interaction with the audience is too much or too little? Fifth, what types of interactions are appropriate and inappropriate? These are just a handful of questions to consider when determining how you communicate your message.

I would be remiss if I did not discuss the trite and inappropriate ways of interacting with the audience that did not truly edify the audience but rather irritate them or be used to manipulate them. First, the mindless repetition of words and phrases. Asking people to repeat a word or phrase is appropriate for school children but is rarely necessary for adults. Second, the raising of hands. Although this can be effective at times, it is often unnecessary. Additionally, many people won't raise their hands today or will lift them to comply with the request, which ultimately becomes an inaccurate poll. Third, asking people to turn to one another and repeat a word or phrase. How sincere and genuine can someone's words be if commanded to say them?

At the heart of this discussion is your view of God's word and your position before God and His sheep. Consider the weight of your responsibility to communicate the text to the audience in an engaging and edifying way, with the end goal of God being exalted in worship. It's essential to connect with the audience; there are many ways to do so, but it must be authentic. Just ensure that your motive and means come from a spirit of grace, truth, and sincerity.

Exercise

First, determine your pulpit preference, one-way or two-way communication with the audience. Second, identify areas in your sermon where one can invite audience participation.

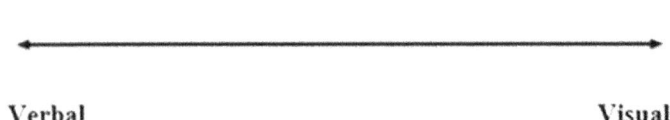

5. *Connection*

Our fifth and final category is to guide your use of media. Today there are many ways to engage your audience visually and audibly. It's essential at the outset to argue that an effective communicator of God's word does not need anything but the Biblical text. However, few preachers are gifted sufficiently to engage a modern mind with a verbal-only presentation. The adage, "a picture is worth a thousand words," is still a relevant reminder.

If one is going to engage with media, one must count the cost. Although many services and tools can simplify the process and bring to the audience high-quality visuals, one must consider the infrastructure and personal expenses to implement and maintain the media experience week-in and week-out. Media can use significant time and resources to prepare and present. Additionally, one must beware of the technical failures that plague any presentation. One must always be ready to "go it alone" if there is an "outage." An unplanned failure can distract the speaker and the audience from the primary message.

Lastly, it is advisable to take the minimalist approach and ensure the message at its core is engaging, effective, and sustainable without all the "bells and whistles." One must not lose sight that the use of media can dull the intellect and imagination of the audience as well as downgrade the communication skills of the preacher and teacher. I suggest reviewing the principles of using illustrations as they apply to media use. Furthermore, there are several questions that I continually ask about whether to use or not use media. First, will people be unclear about the idea if I don't use the media? Second, if the media fails to show, what would I say in its place, and would those words be a sufficient substitute for the media choice? Third, does the media reveal something that words cannot? Fourth, will the media re-engage the audience in a meaningful way? Fifth, am I using the media more than preparing the message?

Exercise

Examine your last five sermons and see if the media would have made the message clearer and more memorable. If you are using media for your sermons, ask how the message would change if the media were unavailable. What changes to the message would you have to make to accommodate this loss?

RECOMMENDED BOOKS

- Anderson, Kenton C. *Choosing to Preach: A Comprehensive Introduction to Sermon Options and Structures*. Grand Rapids, MI: Zondervan Publishing House, 2006.

- Carter, Joe, and John Coleman. *How to Argue like Jesus: Learning Persuasion from History's Greatest Communicator.* Wheaton, IL: Crossway, 2009.
- Decker, Bert, and Hershael W. York. *Speaking with Bold Assurance: How to Become a Persuasive Communicator.* Nashville, TN: Broadman & Holman Publishers, 2001.
- Fishbook, Grant. *How to Communicate Effectively to Modern Audiences.* Logos Mobile Education. Bellingham, WA: Lexham Press, 2018.
- Hughes, Jack. *Expository Preaching with Word Pictures.* Scotland, UK: Christian Focus, 2014.
- Jensen, Richard A. *Envisioning the Word: The Use of Visual Images in Preaching.* Minneapolis, MN: Fortress Press, 2005.
- Koller, Charles W. *How to Preach without Notes.* Grand Rapids, MI: Baker Books, 2007.

- Newman, Mark; Ogle, Donna. *Visual Literacy: Reading, Thinking, and Communicating with Visuals.* Lanham, MD: Rowman & Littlefield Publishers, 2019.
- Overstreet, R. Larry. *Persuasive Preaching: A Biblical and Practical Guide to the Effective Use of Persuasion.* Bellingham, WA: Lexham Press, 2014.
- Schultze, Quentin J., and Diane M. Badzinski. *An Essential Guide to Interpersonal Communication: Building Great Relationships with Faith, Skill, and Virtue in the Age of Social Media.* Grand Rapids, MI: Baker Academic, 2015.

CHAPTER FOURTEEN

DROP ANCHOR! DEALING WITH DEEP AND DIFFICULT PASSAGES

"As also in all his epistles, speaking in them of these things; in which are some things hard to be understood, which they that are unlearned and unstable wrest, as they do also the other Scriptures, unto their own destruction."

— Peter the Apostle, 2 Peter 3:16

PURPOSE

Learn principles to help you work through difficult passages and remain biblical.

INSTRUCTION

Difficult passages are both thrilling and terrifying. They are the objects of unbelievers' attacks. They can be enigmas that perplex us, but difficult texts should never leave us doubting our God or His word. There are very few uncrackable passages in the Scriptures, but there are many passages where one text component may be baffling. For example, Genesis 6:1-4 describes the sons of God and the Nephilim. With a bit of in-depth study, one can resolve the identity of the 'sons of God.' But the Nephilim and, in particular, their nature…well, that's a bit more challenging. It's unavoidable…you will come across difficult passages, but passages like these are more the exception than the rule.

Another challenging passage is Exodus 4:19–26. In Exodus 4:24, the expression "the Lord met him, and sought to put him to death." The difficulty in this passage is first, who is "him" and second, why would the Lord seek to kill? Passages like this can be a source of stumbling. An incorrect conclusion can sometimes lead to errant thinking and even heresy. We must tread carefully!

With this in mind, I hope the following steps will provide a framework that will lead to illumination, not confusion, understanding rather than misunderstanding, and narrowing down the possible interpretations rather than leaving them open-ended with too many options. This chapter provides two lists, each with a specific purpose. The first list is to guide you in working through a difficult passage. The second list is to guide you in your conversations with others regarding controversial texts.

Steps for Studying Difficult and Controversial Passages

Step 0: Begin with Prayer

Our ability to comprehend and apprehend the Word of God is only possible through the Holy Spirit. If we go to God in humility asking for illumination, if we study to show ourselves approved as a workman who does not be ashamed, and if we enlist the help of others, our Lord will provide us the understanding we need or at least help us know when we can go no further.

Step 1: Translate the text from the original language & Consult several English translations

As mentioned in previous chapters, without access to the original language, the reader loses precision through the translation. Many texts are simply misunderstood because the English translation does not accurately reflect the meaning and grammar of the original language text. Therefore, one must get to the source to understand what the author intended.

Step 2: Do a concordance search on every word in the OT and NT

Many controversies are connected to a particular word or phrase. By examining all the contexts, one can derive a better range of meanings and determine how to interpret a passage more precisely. This task is especially important with subject and verb relationships. As you look at each word used, be sure to look at each context and determine the meaning for each context. That will help eliminate the possible interpretations.

Step 3: Do a word study for each word: checking dictionaries and lexicons

A word study is in order if a particular word is critical for understanding a passage. Besides thoroughly studying a word's use in Biblical contexts, it may be necessary to study its use outside of Scripture. You should consult at least three dictionaries. Additionally, be mindful that the immediate context determines the final meaning of a word or phrase.

Step 4: Identify the grammatical issues: Identify phrases, word relationships within the verse and immediate context

Word meaning is ultimately determined by its specific use within a particular context. This is why one must incorporate the rules of grammar in one's studies to ensure the right understanding. Grammar rules can sometimes rule out or reinforce a particular meaning crucial for insight. Through a process of elimination, one can get closer to the meaning. Grammar studies are especially difficult if you don't have original language training. However, many good grammars don't require Hebrew and Greek expertise, but using grammar resources requires understanding grammatical insights. You may need to research further online to understand grammatical concepts discussed in grammatical books.

Step 5: Understand the circles of context (before/after verse, paragraph, chapter, book, OT/NT books)

Context is king, and many misunderstandings of Scripture are due to not rightly understanding the full and proper context. Contexts will range from the phrase to the sentence to the paragraph to the chapter and even extend to the whole book. One must guard against taking a word or phrase out of its context or inserting a meaning that is foreign to the text and the original author's intended meaning.

Step 6: Identify key cross-references: word, phrase, and topic

Scripture is the best interpreter of Scripture. So many truths are repeated in the Scripture to reinforce and refine the meaning. To avoid misinterpretation, one must rightly determine the related passages to guide the reader to all the pertinent and relevant information for accurate interpretation. Very few passages genuinely stand alone in meaning and content. There is usually a parallel passage, a complimentary passage, or even a portion of the idea found elsewhere that can guide the interpretation.

Step 7: Develop the internal/Biblical outline from the text: Identify the flow of the story, argument, and/or key thoughts

Determining the structure of the text is critical for unlocking its meaning in a text. For example, when studying the book of Proverbs, parallelism is one of the keys to interpreting these pithy sayings. By aligning what is in parallel, examining if a pair of words or phrases are synonymous or opposite in meaning can be the crucial key to unlocking the precise interpretation of the text. Depending on the genre of the text, there are other structures to examine: chiastic structures, rhetorical structures, story structures, etc.

Step 8: Write out what you believe the text is saying
Expressing your conclusions in writing is essential to bring more precision to your thoughts. Additionally, make sure you have evidence of your findings. As a last step, take the time to compare your position to the interpretations found in various commentators, looking for what is similar and dissimilar.

Step 9: Create a pro/con argument
This step is absolutely critical for complex issues. By organizing your ideas by the arguments that support the idea and the arguments that reject the idea, you will be in a far better position to see the strengths and weaknesses of your conclusions objectively. This process can be time-consuming and requires effort to think from both sides of the argument. However, this will allow you to handle new information and those opposing your analysis and conclusions. With your

pro/con structure in hand, any new information can be applied, and then one can objectively reevaluate the previous conclusions. This strategy is the surest way to remain objective and open-minded to new evidence.

Step 10: Consult exegetical commentaries, theology books, scholarly journals, history, and other well-argued positions

These resources provide a plethora of information from various positions to help you consider your view from all angles. Collecting resources that reason well with documented evidence is vital, even if their opinions differ from your current conclusions. Examining the arguments and corresponding evidence will make it easier to determine whether you have interpreted rightly and if your evidence is sufficient to maintain your interpretative decision and conclusion.

Step 11: Weigh the evidence

This step requires objectivity as well as being analytical. You need to determine if the evidence is adequate, and you will have to prioritize the evidence and rank its importance and relevance to your arguments and conclusions. Just because you think you have a great point does not mean it's the best "leg to stand on."

Step 12: Arrive at a studied conclusion
By this stage, you know why you believe what you believe. If you have been thorough in your analysis up to this point, your argument should be able to withstand opposing arguments, but more importantly, you will be confident that your interpretation is correct. Although new evidence and arguments may appear, you will have the means to re-evaluate them objectively. Ultimately, you will continue to pursue the truth rather than allow personal feelings or bias to become the blind spot to a more precise interpretation and conclusion.

Steps for Discussing Difficult and Controversial Passages
This last section of our current chapter will help you to

examine yourself and ensure you proceed with humility, open-mindedness, discernment, and being wise and balanced in your words and ways. Keep in mind Solomon's wisdom, particularly from Proverbs 26:4-5, which reminds us there is a time to remain silent and a time to speak. May you discern the difference:

Proverbs 26:4–5

4 Do not answer a fool according to his folly,

Or you will also be like him.

5 Answer a fool as his folly deserves,

That he not be wise in his own eyes.

Ground Zero: Have you prayed?

- Without prayer, you will not have the Spirit's help nor be fully equipped in the right frame of mind to engage. Make prayer a priority.

Question #1: Is this a controversial passage?

- Avoid creating a conflict where there is none and understand that if many reputable scholars highly dispute an interpretation, one should be cautious about being dogmatic. However, if the evidence points to a particular position, in humility, hold to the most Biblical position.

Question #2: Is the view being explained one of the main/traditional views or something non-traditional?

- It's important to separate what is in the realm of Biblical truth versus a new and novel view not grounded in Scripture. Don't give up ground to a position that contradicts the Scriptures or is outside the realm of Biblical orthodoxy.

Question #3: Are the major views being explained?

- If someone is ignoring a significant view and hiding the evidence, this must be pointed out. If one does not understand the basic arguments and positions, it might be best not to proceed until those issues are addressed.

Question #4: Has the speaker and you both prayed and studied the passage in-depth as a good Berean?

- Without someone doing their due diligence and seeking help from the spirit, there is the potential for the flesh to interfere and undermine the pursuit of truth. Of course, this goes both ways for all those debating Scripture.

Question #5: Does the view taught conflict with another fundamental doctrine?

- This situation can be difficult to discern, but one must not carefully agree with any point that conflicts with Biblical truth. This kind of compromise can undermine any argument and conclusion. No matter how small or innocuous, a conclusion with a false premise or an argument not grounded in truth is a house of cards that will eventually collapse in time.

Question #6: Is this passage truly resolvable?

- The scripture reveals in Deuteronomy 29:29 "The secret things belong to the LORD our God, but the things revealed belong to us and to our sons forever, that we may observe all the words of this law." Pursuing the "impossible to know" will only lead to frustration or speculation, and neither will find validation. There are not too many "Gordian Knots" in Scripture, but one must discern when a passage is not resolvable.

Question #7: Are you willing to speak one-on-one about the passage with a desire to learn rather than argue?

- This step is an important test of the heart and attitude. If one seeks only to argue rather than resolve, then an impasse is at hand, and no good can come from two people arguing from a position where no ground will be given up.

Question #8: Is it worth confronting this issue?

- Sometimes, issues will take care of themselves, or the matter is so trivial that it's not worth engaging in or pursuing. One must avoid nitpicking and wisely choose when to engage.

Question #9: After speaking one-on-one, are you able to discuss this with others without creating division or slandering someone; can you walk away from a disagreement in love?

This question is another crucial test—the test of love for others versus the love for self and ego. The former will keep the peace, and the latter will result in conflict. Paul's admonition in Galatians 5:15, "But if you bite and devour one another, take care that you are not consumed by one another," is an excellent reminder to guard against the ungodly actions flowing from pride that will destroy relationships.

In closing, consider the following passages:

- **Proverbs 18:17** "The first to plead his case seems right, until another comes and examines him."

- **Matthew 18:15–17** "If your brother sins, go and show him his fault in private; if he listens to you, you have won your brother. But if he does not listen to you, take one or two more with you, so that BY

THE MOUTH OF TWO OR THREE WITNESSES EVERY FACT MAY BE CONFIRMED. If he refuses to listen to them, tell it to the church; and if he refuses to listen even to the church, let him be to you as a Gentile and a tax collector."

- **Ephesians 5:17–21** "So then do not be foolish, but understand what the will of the Lord is. And do not get drunk with wine, for that is dissipation, but be filled with the Spirit, speaking to one another in psalms and hymns and spiritual songs, singing and making melody with your heart to the Lord; always giving thanks for all things in the name of our Lord Jesus Christ to God, even the Father; and be subject to one another in the fear of Christ."
- **James 3:1–18** "Let not many of you become teachers, my brethren, knowing that as such we will incur a stricter judgment. For we all stumble in many ways. If anyone does not stumble in what he says, he is a perfect man, able to bridle the whole

body as well. Now if we put the bits into the horses' mouths so that they will obey us, we direct their entire body as well. Look at the ships also, though they are so great and are driven by strong winds, are still directed by a very small rudder wherever the inclination of the pilot desires. So also the tongue is a small part of the body, and yet it boasts of great things. See how great a forest is set aflame by such a small fire! And the tongue is a fire, the very world of iniquity; the tongue is set among our members as that which defiles the entire body, and sets on fire the course of our life, and is set on fire by hell. For every species of beasts and birds, of reptiles and creatures of the sea, is tamed and has been tamed by the human race. But no one can tame the tongue; it is a restless evil and full of deadly poison. With it we bless our Lord and Father, and with it we curse men, who have been made in the likeness of God; from the same mouth come both blessing and cursing. My brethren, these things ought not to be this way. Does a fountain send out from the same opening both fresh and bitter water? Can a fig tree, my brethren, produce olives, or a vine produce figs? Nor can salt water produce fresh. Who among you is wise and understanding? Let him show by his good behavior his deeds in the gentleness of wisdom. But if you have bitter jealousy and selfish ambition in your heart, do not be arrogant and so lie against the truth. This wisdom is not that which comes down from above, but is earthly, natural, demonic. For where jealousy and selfish ambition exist, there is disorder and every evil thing. But the wisdom from above is first pure, then peaceable, gentle, reasonable, full of mercy and good fruits, unwavering, without hypocrisy. And the seed whose fruit is righteousness is sown in peace by those who make peace.

RECOMMENDED BOOKS

- Zondervan Counterpoints Series (41 vols.) (Zondervan)
- Spectrum Multiview Book Series (27 vols.) (IVP Academic)
- Perspectives Series (9 vols.) (B&H)
- Perspectives Series (4 vols.) (B&H)
- Zondervan Counterpoints Series (35 vols.)

DIGITAL SWORD

CHAPTER FIFTEEN

GOING MOBILE

"But thou, O Daniel, shut up the words, and seal the book, even to the time of the end: many shall run to and fro, and knowledge shall be increased."

— Daniel the Prophet, Daniel 12:4

PURPOSE

Learn to leverage your mobile Bible software tools for worship, Bible Study, and Bible memorization when your laptop or desktop is unavailable.

PREPARATION

There are a variety of mobile Bible apps and tools for phones and tablets. Although it is impossible to list them all here, we'll provide a list of applications worth investigating. Please see the end of the chapter for a list of mobile applications available.

INSTRUCTION

In addition to mobile apps, while writing this book, AI artificial intelligence tools have been made available to the marketplace. These, too, can be used for Biblical research. Tools like ChatGPT, Gemini, Claude, and Llama are just the beginning of the AI revolution that is taking place around us. Many of these tools are two-tier: a free and a fee-based version. Currently, I am using several fee-based pro-versions for faster answers and more options. These tools are so easy to use because you can ask nearly any question, and they will provide answers to secular and spiritual topics in an easy-to-understand response.

These AI tools are a lot of fun and engaging, too. For my experiment with AI, I completed my research before using this tool. I began by asking ChatGPT what it thought the top ten features of mobile Bible software were to see if the results aligned and matched with previous research and knowledge on this topic. It answered the question so wonderfully that I asked for ten more features. With this in mind and so that you can see the AI firsthand, I will provide a list of those 20 features provided by the AI below. However, I have modified the order and descriptions to personalize the material for this chapter.

TOP 20 FEATURES AND BENEFITS

Disclaimer: Not every app has all these features, but this is a composite picture combining all the elements across a spectrum of various mobile software. Additionally, the order of the list is not ranked.

Study Tools

- Mobile apps have streamlined their features to accomplish a study task more quickly and efficiently with a tap or swipe. For example, Bible Word studies, note-taking tools, Bible concordance searching, and accessing commentaries are just some of the tools to help you go deeper into God's Word.

Searching

- Each application is a little different, but the search

engines in the mobile apps will help you find related passages quickly, simplifying the process of finding Scriptures connected to the topic you are studying. There is no better interpreter of the Bible than the Bible. Many advanced mobile apps can search non-bible resources such as commentaries, word study dictionaries, and much more. Additionally, some tools can search not only on Strong's numbers but in the original language for Hebrew, Aramaic, and Greek word searches.

Multiple Bible Translations

- It's standard today for most Bible software to include several free Bible translations. Some platforms will charge a small fee for additional and specialized translations.

Bible Comparison

- There are several tools that will make it easier to compare one Bible translation with another. Consulting several translations can help you understand the meaning better, but the word changes can be a signal to look up a particular word.

Audio Features
- As mobile apps take advantage of text-to-speech technology, it is becoming increasingly easier to have any book in your digital library read to you. Usually, one can control the voice and speed to help one listen faster. By the way, I recommend increasing your listening speed once every 14 sessions. You will be surprised how quickly your hearing will adjust, and soon you'll be able to save even more time and still have excellent comprehension.

Diverse Resources
- The digital library offerings found in mobile apps continue to expand and increase. No longer are Bible apps simply Bibles, commentaries, and dictionaries. They include maps, charts, theological

journals, audiobooks, and so much more.

Diverse Reporting

- Due to the smaller screen sizes, these applications have had to retool and present information in a more user-friendly way. This change has made the information more engaging and easier to read.

Ease of Use

- Mobile apps are continuing to innovate to make content more engaging to read and easier to navigate. This reduces the number of steps to search and find information and makes tools more user-friendly, helping users study more effectively.

Customization & Personalization

- The mobile applications allow users to change colors, font size, background, and more. This capability makes Bible reading easier on the eyes. This visual help is a real benefit for those who need a large print or high-contrast color scheme. Additionally, some mobile software allows one to save multiple study layouts or leverage the "favorites feature" to make recalling a book, tool, or specialized search easier.

Worship and Devotion
- Whether you prefer an actual devotional book that is calendar-based or create your own reading plan of a specific book for encouragement and spiritual growth, it is now possible to do both in mobile software.

2Dos and Tracking
- More and more applications have reminders, daily and weekly study series to help get you in the habit of spending time memorizing, meditating, and meeting the Lord in prayer. This help is a beautiful way to build good study habits. Additionally, to avoid falling behind, there are reminders to encourage your progress.

Share and Social

- It is now possible and easier to share what you are learning and doing inside your mobile apps with others. The capabilities include sharing with another person, a small group, or your favorite social media accounts.

Offline Convenience
- Mobile tools are wonderful when you have an excellent cellular or WIFI connection, but what do you do on airplanes or when there is a weak or no signal available? Some apps now permit you to save and download for offline use. Of course, always ensure you have enough space on your device before downloading a lot of information.

Free and Nearly Free
- Even though the robust mobile applications will charge you for additional features and resources, many of these companies offer a lite version with a handful of free resources and tools. This first step is a great way to test an application and 'try before

you buy.'

Synchronization

- One of the best features is the information syncing between my desktop and my mobile devices. The instant, seamless sharing of information between devices has saved me time and given me more flexibility to study and learn.

PRESENTATION

- https://www.DigitalSword.org/mobile
- This training video will overview the Logos Mobile application for the IOS and the web-based application.

RECOMMENDED MOBILE APPLICATIONS

Accordance (Bible Study)

- https://www.accordancebible.com/accordance-for-android/
- https://www.accordancebible.com/accordance-mobile/

Bible Gateway App (Bible Study)

- https://www.biblegateway.com/app/

Bible Memory

- https://biblememory.com/

Blue Letter Bible (Bible Study)

- https://www.blueletterbible.org/apps-tools.cfm

Christian Audio (Audio Books)

- https://christianaudio.com

Dwell (Audio Bible)

- https://dwellapp.io/

eSword (Bible Study)

- https://www.e-sword.net/iphone/

- https://www.e-sword.net/ipad/

Faith Comes by Hearing (Audio Bible)

- https://www.faithcomesbyhearing.com/audio-bible-resources

Fighter Verses: Memorize Bible

- https://www.fighterverses.com/tools

Filament (Bible Study)

- https://www.tyndale.com/sites/filamentbibleexperience/

Got Questions? (Bible Questions and Answers)

- https://www.gotquestions.org/

Logos Mobile Application (Bible Study)

- Mobile: https://www.logos.com/bible-app

- Web-Based: https://app.logos.com

Olive Tree Bible Apps (Bible Study)

- https://www.olivetree.com/

Our Daily Bread (Devotions)

- https://ourdailybread.org/mobileresources/

Proclaim (Presenter Software)

- https://faithlife.com/products/proclaim

- The mobile app lets you view and control the desktop presenter software.

Sermon Audio

- https://www.sermonaudio.com/mobile.asp

Tecarta Bible (Bible Study)

- https://tecartabible.com/home

- https://play.google.com/store/apps/details?id=com.tecarta.TecartaBible

- https://apps.apple.com/us/app/tecarta-bible/id325955298

VCY America (Christian Content)

- https://www.vcyamerica.org/radio/get-the-vcy-mobile-app/

You Version (Bible Study)

- https://www.youversion.com/the-bible-app/

CHAPTER SIXTEEN

GOD, YOU, & AI: BIBLE STUDY & SERMON PREPARATION

"And he had power to give life unto the image of the beast, that the image of the beast should both speak, and cause that as many as would not worship the image of the beast should be killed."

— John the Apostle, Revelation 13:15

INTRODUCTION

The passage above speaks of a future time called the Tribulation. What exactly is the image of the beast that it can be given life, speak, and cause those to refuse its worship to be killed is challenging to know in our current place in time. However, technology will undoubtedly be a tool of the antichrist, but until then, what role can technology serve in the church age? Can such tools and tech be used to further Christ's Gospel, His church, and your ministry?

If one is to answer in the affirmative, we must proceed

with wisdom and caution to understand the inherent risks of using these digital tools. Due to the significant scope of such a topic, our discussion will be limited to using artificial intelligence for Bible study and sermon preparation and addressing the concern of plagiarism.

RISKS

The number one temptation of AI is its ease of use for plagiarizing. Even before AI, far too many leaders in the church had taken credit for another person's work. I have witnessed firsthand a pastor, on regular occasions, take multiple paragraphs of commentaries and insert them word for word in their sermon, without citation, and preach from the pulpit as if it were their words and work. This is egregious, sinful, and, frankly, disqualifying.

Let's be clear: we are not talking about using someone else's illustration, story, or quote, although those should also be cited. However, when someone repeats the logic, arguments, and full context of another, it is no longer the spiritual byproduct of the leader's labor in prayer and personal study. Instead, it is a lazy shortcut and an ethical breach of trust between God and the congregation.

AI can be a vehicle for plagiarism on a whole new level. It is possible to generate a full sermon nearly indistinguishable from a manually created message. The implications of utilizing AI in this fashion are significant. Consider the following three costs: conscience, congregation, and the condemned.

First, the personal cost to conscience cannot be fully measured. James 3:1 speaks of a stricter judgment for teachers, and Titus 1:5–9 outlines the qualifications of a spiritual leader, including not being fond of sordid gain and holding fast to the faithful word. Paul exhorts Timothy in 2 Timothy 2:15 "Study to shew thyself approved unto God, a workman that needeth not to be ashamed, rightly dividing the word of truth." Using AI-generated sermons violates all these exhortations and commandments. Such a violation will forsake one's future heavenly rewards.

One of the many benefits of studying and preparing a message is the personal refreshment, renewal, and reminder of the word in the minister's life. Such a process sanctifies, reproves, rebukes, recalls, and reaffirms the truths that one must steward personally for holiness and Christ-like growth (2 Timothy 4:1–2). Additionally, how can one truly minister to another if they are a hollow preacher simply serving up the work of another?

Second, there is a cost to the congregation. The church must be fed God's word, from the "pure milk of the word" for newborn babes (1 Peter 2:2) to the "solid food" for the mature (Hebrews 5:13–14). Without the regular intake of the clear, accurate, in-depth exposition of God's word, the congregation becomes weak, loses discernment, stunted in their growth, and becomes unholy and unfaithful to their Savior. Ministry will fail, and those under such teaching will fail to fulfill their calling, utilize their gifts, evangelize, and truly worship. One only needs to look at Revelation 2-3 to see the devasting effects when Christ and His word are no longer central to His people.

Third, there is a cost to the condemned. We know that if one has not believed in Jesus Christ, they have been judged because they have not believed in the name of the only begotten son of God (John 3:16-18). Paul in Romans 10:14 states, "How then shall they call on him in whom they have not believed? And how shall they believe in him of whom they have not heard? And how shall they hear without a preacher?" AI-generated messages are no substitute for the authentic preaching of God's word to evangelize the lost.

A weak church will drift into worldliness, no longer salt and light, to a lost and dying world that desperately needs to taste and see the Lord is good. Should a lost person find their way into a worldly church with a hollow preacher, the AI artificial message may arouse the flesh and the emotions, but it cannot awaken the dead soul in its trespasses and sins (Ephesians 2:1-10). This is just a cursory look at the implications of replacing a spirit-man-generated message with an AI-man-generated message. It does not take much imagination to understand the pitfalls and problems of being dependent upon a tool that is often run by individuals who are non-Christian in their worldviews. However, one must also recognize that, like many tools, AI may be a help or hindrance based on who uses it, how they use it, and why they use it. Let's consider the ethical uses of AI for Bible study and sermon preparation.

ETHICS

AI has many capabilities that can assist in the study and accurate exegesis of the biblical text. I recommend checking out my webinar, 10 Practical and Ethical Uses of Chat GPT4 for Bible Study and Sermon Preparation. You can purchase and download it from my website: https://www.learnlogos.com/chatgpt_p/chatgpt.htm.

One can train AI to follow specific methodologies for inductive Bible study and exegetical and theological analysis. The AI tools are improving their ability to summarize large amounts of information and even organize it into tables for a more straightforward presentation of the data. AI can produce original language analysis, including textual, lexical, morphological, and grammatical analysis. It can discover chiastic structures, parallelism, and other structures within the Biblical text.

Another important aspect of Bible study is exploring the historical background of a text. AI has access to extensive records of the past, which can be searched and retrieved. This is a far superior way to find relevant historical information than traditional Google searching. Theological analysis is another surprising capability of artificial intelligence. It is possible to train AI to understand the theological categories mentioned in Chapter 7 and identify the predominant theological themes of any passage.

One particular use of AI that I frequently use is finding cross-references. Although one can search by a word and phrase from the Biblical text if known, AI can search thematically or conceptually when you don't know the word or phrase from the Biblical text. For example, one could prompt AI to find passages related to "financial stewardship." This is a difficult search for Bible software, although it is possible to find such passages with the right digital resources by employing several search strategies.

One of my favorite use cases for AI is constructing pro-con analysis tables from various resources with differing hermeneutical methodologies and theological presuppositions. Not only is this easy, but it is a lot of fun and illuminating. AI can even convert the information into a memorable study framework using mnemonics.

Another helpful use case for AI is constructing relevant illustrations and applications. One can utilize a multitude of illustrations and applications from paper or digital resources and allow the AI to repurpose them for the passage being examined and contemporized for the current audience. It may require a bit of back-and-forth interaction with the AI to achieve a helpful anecdote, but with some effort, the resulting outcome is usually useful and relevant.

It is impossible to exhaust the multitude of ways one can apply AI. One is only limited by their imagination. Whether you use AI to improve your writing style with better word choices like a thesaurus or improve your writing style like Grammarly, consider AI as your go-to expert to assist. But remember, always, always, always examine the results. AI is known to hallucinate, invent information, and make wrong conclusions and associations. So, use it with wisdom and discernment.

How to Use AI for Bible Study and Sermon Preparation Ethically

In wrapping up this final chapter, I would like to provide a series of "AI prompts" so you can experiment with AI to discover its capabilities and usefulness for Bible Study and sermon preparation. The following prompts were utilized with OpenAI ChatGPT 4: https://chatgpt.com.

1. Prayer

a. Use the prayer template of Jesus in Matthew 6:9–13 (copy and paste the prayer into the AI prompt), can you list several prayer prompts connected to Mat 25:1-13?

b. Here is the outline of Dr. John Fallahee's book on prayer "REFLECT the glory of God in prayer."

Step 1 - Remember the Glories of God

Step 2 - Examine your Motives & Manner

Step 3 - Face Life with the Scriptures

Step 4 - Love God & Love People

Step 5 - Expect Suffering & Persecution

Step 6 - Concern Yourself with God's Kingdom

Step 7 - Take Every Opportunity

c. Can you create prayer based on the steps in the book informed by Matthew 25:1-13?

2. Observing

a. Using the 5Ws & H (who, what, where, when, why, and how), can you generate a list of inductive-based questions that are necessary to investigate Matthew 25:1-13 thoroughly?

b. Are there any literary devices used in Matthew 25:1-13?

c. Is there a literary structure to Matthew 25:1-13?

d. Is there a chiastic structure to Matthew 25:1-13?

e. What are the 10 most significant words in Matthew 25:1-13?

f. What are the 10 most significant phrases in Matthew 25:1-13?

g. What is the near and far context for Matthew 25:1-13?

h. Can you list for me all the contrasts in Matthew 25:1-13?

i. Can you list all the parallelisms at the word, phrase, and sentence level for Matthew 25:1-13?

j. Can you list all the parallelisms at the word, phrase, and sentence level in the Greek for Matthew 25:1-13?

3. Outlining

a. Can you outline Matthew 25:1-13 based on the verbs?

b. Can you outline Matthew 25:1-13 based on the subjects?

c. Can you outline Matthew 25:1-13 based on underlying Greek primary clauses?

d. Can you create a thematic outline from the text of Matthew 25:1-13?

e. Can you provide the socio-rhetorical structure of Matthew 25:1-13 similar to Ben Witherington?

4. Word Study

a. Can you give me a list of repeated Greek words in Matthew 25:1-13?

b. Can you rank the topmost key Greek words for Matthew 25:1-13 based on their use in the text?

c. Is there anything morphologically significant in the Greek text for Matthew 25:1-13?

d. Can you give me the definition of φρόνιμος keeping

the context of Matthew 25:1-13?

e. Is this Greek word used in the LXX, and what is its related Hebrew word?

5. Grammar Study

a. Can you give me a grammatical layout of Matthew 25:1 in a table format, including the Greek word, Greek transliteration, and English, as well as notes on parts of speech with morphological information?

b. Are there any significant grammatical constructions that are noteworthy and contribute to the overall meaning and structure of Matthew 25:1-13?

c. Are there any grammatical figures of speech in Matthew 25:1-13?

d. Are there any significant prepositional phrases based on the Greek in Matthew 25:1-13?

6. Cross-Referencing

a. Can you give me the 10 most significant bible cross references related to Matthew 25:1-13?

b. Can you give me any cross references from the book of Proverbs related to Matthew 25:1-13?

c. Can you give me an intertextual reference from the Old Testament to Matthew 25:1-13?

d. Can you give me cross-references that contrast Matthew 25:1-13?

7. Historical Background

a. What significant historical background elements are essential to understanding Matthew 25:1-13?

b. Can you provide the biblical historical background on lamps from Matthew 25:1-13?

c. Can you provide the biblical historical background on virgins for Matthew 25:1-13?

d. Can you provide the biblical historical background on purchasing oil for Matthew 25:1-13?

8. Theological Background

a. Here are 13 Great Themes of the Bible:

1. Scripture/Bibliology

2. God the Father / Theology

3. God the Son / Christology

4. God the Spirit / Pneumatology

5. Creation / Cosmology (Material / Spiritual)

6. Angels / Angelology

7. Satan - Demons / Demonology

8. Man / Anthropology

9. Sin / Hamartiology

10. Salvation / Soteriology

11. Israel / Israelology

12. Church / Ecclesiology

13. End Times / Eschatology

b. Based on the list of theological themes provided, can you analyze Matthew 25:1-11 and rank these themes from the most frequently referenced to the least frequently referenced?

9. Cross-Checking

a. In a table format, can you give me no more than 10 symbols with 3 possible interpretations of the key symbols found in Matthew 25:1-13?

b. Can you give me a table with the top 10 key symbols in a column for interpretation, and, in the columns to the right, provide pro and con arguments for interpreting the symbols found in Matthew 25:1-13?

c. In a table format, can you list the 10 symbols in Matthew 25:1-13 and then, in the columns to the right, provide the top 3 interpretations ranked, with an exegetical reason for each interpretation?

10. Illustration

a. Can you provide a modern-day illustration using the framework of Matthew 25:1-13?

b. Can you give me a four-sentence modern-day illustration of Matthew 25:1-13?

c. Can you give me a single sentence of a modern-day simile, metaphor, and analogy based on the theme of being prepared and not being prepared from Matthew 25:1-13 in a table format noting the category?

11. Application

a. In a table format, can you provide five spiritual applications from Matthew 25:1-13 for being prepared and not being prepared, and in the three columns to the right, have a spiritual application for thinking, speaking, and doing, providing Biblical cross reference for each application?

Conclusion

As you can see, the possibility of leveraging AI for Biblical and theological analysis is quite promising. Although one may be limited in skill and knowledge in various areas related to hermeneutics, exegesis, history, Bible study, and more, AI can come alongside and be a helpful tool to supplement and lend a hand. It is my hope that we never lose sight of our dependence upon prayer, hard work, and especially the Holy Spirit for illumination and discovery. May you wisely utilize these tools with caution and spiritual discernment!

ABOUT THE AUTHOR

In 1995, author John David Fallahee was delivered from bondage to alcohol and drugs by his Lord and Savior, Jesus Christ. Through prayer, studying the Scriptures, and discipleship in the local church, John found redemption, power, and hope.

This book shares principles he has learned for studying the Word of God with computer software and walking in fear of the Lord and in the comfort of the Holy Spirit.

John is presently serving as pastor at Good News Bible Church in Green Bay, Wisconsin (GoodNewsBC.com) and coaches online (LearnLogos.com).

www.ingramcontent.com/pod-product-compliance
Lightning Source LLC
Chambersburg PA
CBHW052130070526
44585CB00017B/1764